PRESIDENTIAL Trivia

Also by Richard Lederer

Adventures of a Verbivore
Anguished English
The Ants Are My Friends (with Stan Kegel)
Basic Verbal Skills (with Philip Burnham)
The Bride of Anguished English
The Circus of Words
Classic Literary Trivia
Comma Sense (with John Shore)
Crazy English
The Cunning Linguist
Fractured English
Get Thee to a Punnery
The Giant Book of Animal Jokes (with James Ertner)
Have Yourself a Punny Little Christmas
Literary Trivia
A Man of My Words
The Miracle of Language
More Anguished English
The Play of Words
Pun & Games
Puns Spooken Here
The Revenge of Anguished English
Sleeping Dogs Don't Lay (with Richard Dowis)
The Word Circus
Word Play Crosswords, vols. 1 and 2 (with Gayle Dean)
Word Wizard
The Write Way (with Richard Dowis)

Presidential Trivia

RICHARD LEDERER

ILLUSTRATIONS BY
ART PARTS AND
BLACK EYE DESIGN

The
Feats, Fates,
Families, Foibles,
and Firsts of Our
American
Presidents

Gibbs Smith, Publisher

TO ENRICH AND INSPIRE HUMANKIND

Salt Lake City | Charleston | Santa Fe | Santa Barbara

TO JEANNE JENSEN, SISTER OF THE HEART

First Edition
12 11 10 09 08   7 6 5 4 3

Published by
Gibbs Smith, Publisher
P.O. Box 667
Layton, Utah 84041

Orders: 1.800.835.4993
www.gibbs-smith.com

Designed by Black Eye Design (blackeye.com)
Printed and bound in Canada

Library of Congress Cataloging-in-Publication Data
       Library of Congress Control Number: 2007932213
ISBN 13: 978-1-4236-0210-2
ISBN 10: 1-4236-0210-1

CONTENTS

INTRODUCTION

WHEN GEORGE WASHINGTON BECAME PRESIDENT in 1789, other national leaders included the king of France, the czarina of Russia, the emperor of China, and the shogun of Japan. Today, no king rules France, no czar rules Russia, no emperor rules China, and no shogun rules Japan. But the office of President of the United States endures.

"When I was a boy I was told that anybody could become President; I'm beginning to believe it," quipped Clarence Darrow. Very few nations have a governmental system that allows *anyone* to become the leader of the country, in this case, the most powerful in the world. Our presidents have been highly educated and barely schooled: Woodrow Wilson earned a Ph.D. in political science from Johns Hopkins University, while Andrew Johnson never attended school but was trained as a garment maker and wore only suits that he himself had custom tailored.

Our presidents have been filthy rich and dirt poor, generals and civilians, professional politicians and utter amateurs, sober as a judge and drunk as a skunk, eloquent and barely articulate, handsome and plug-ugly. In the past century alone, the White House has been occupied by the son of a Presbyterian minister, a schoolteacher, a peanut farmer, a failed haberdasher, a former actor, and the son of a failed California lemon rancher.

The framers of the Constitution could not have envisioned the power that the president now holds to influence world and domestic affairs. Our fore-

fathers and foremothers could not have dreamt that presidents would be the subjects and objects of so much intense interest in their philosophies, opinions, policies, and personal lives.

Historian Henry Adams, the grandson and great-grandson of presidents, wrote that the president "resembles the commander of a ship at sea. He must have a helm to grasp, a course to steer, a port to seek." The voyages that our American presidents have steered on the ship of state are some of the brightest adventures that any nation has experienced since the dawn of civilization. To begin our exploration of our chief executives, let's review the names of the forty-two men (Grover Cleveland, for some bizarre reason, is traditionally counted twice) who have been President of the United States:

1. George Washington, 1789–1797
2. John Adams, 1797–1801
3. Thomas Jefferson, 1801–1809
4. James Madison, 1809–1817
5. James Monroe, 1817–1825
6. John Quincy Adams, 1825–1829
7. Andrew Jackson, 1829–1837
8. Martin Van Buren, 1837–1841
9. William Henry Harrison, 1841
10. John Tyler, 1841–1845
11. James Knox Polk, 1845–1849
12. Zachary Taylor, 1849–1850
13. Millard Fillmore, 1850–1853
14. Franklin Pierce, 1853–1857
15. James Buchanan, 1857–1861
16. Abraham Lincoln, 1861–1865
17. Andrew Johnson, 1865–1869
18. Ulysses Simpson Grant, 1869–1877
19. Rutherford Birchard Hayes, 1877–1881
20. James Abram Garfield, 1881
21. Chester Alan Arthur, 1881–1885
22. Grover Cleveland, 1885–1889

23. Benjamin Harrison, 1889–1893
24. Grover Cleveland, 1893–1897
25. William McKinley, 1897–1901
26. Theodore Roosevelt, 1901–1909
27. William Howard Taft, 1909–1913
28. Woodrow Wilson, 1913–1921
29. Warren Gamaliel Harding, 1921–1923
30. Calvin Coolidge, 1923–1929
31. Herbert Clark Hoover, 1929–1933
32. Franklin Delano Roosevelt, 1933–1945
33. Harry S. Truman, 1945–1953
34. Dwight David Eisenhower, 1953–1961
35. John Fitzgerald Kennedy, 1961–1963
36. Lyndon Baines Johnson, 1963–1969
37. Richard Milhous Nixon, 1969–1974
38. Gerald Rudolph Ford, 1974–1977
39. James Earl Carter Jr., 1977–1981
40. Ronald Wilson Reagan, 1981–1989
41. George Herbert Walker Bush, 1989–1993
42. William Jefferson Clinton, 1993–2001
43. George Walker Bush, 2001–2008

CHAPTER I.
PRESIDENTIAL PRECEDENTS

WHO WAS THE FIRST PRESIDENT BORN A UNITED STATES CITIZEN?

Martin Van Buren (1837–1841), our eighth president, entered the earthly stage on December 5, 1782, making him the first president born after the Declaration of Independence was signed. Eight presidents were born before 1776 as British subjects—**George Washington, John Adams, Thomas Jefferson, James Madison, James Monroe, John Quincy Adams, Andrew Jackson,** and, after Van Buren, **William Henry Harrison.** To put it another way, seven of our first eight presidents were not born in the United States; they were born in the American Colonies.

WHO WAS THE FIRST PRESIDENT TO BE IMPEACHED?

If you answered **Richard Nixon,** you're mistaken. President Nixon resigned before any impeachment trial. **Andrew Johnson** and **Bill Clinton** were tried under the articles of impeachment. Both were acquitted (Johnson by a single vote in the Senate), but, still, they were both impeached.

QUIZ

First and foremost, here's a quiz about presidential firsts. You can be certain that the answers won't be of the "gotcha!" type that you've just read. If you aren't a fan of quizzes, you can pass Go and leap right to the fascinating answers that follow the fascinating questions in this chapter and the two that follow.

Hint: The answers to the questions are, for the most part, in the order of when each president served.

1. WHO WAS THE FIRST PRESIDENT BORN IN A LOG CABIN?

Andrew Jackson. Although several more have claimed it, there were only five others—**Millard Fillmore, James Buchanan, Abraham Lincoln, Andrew Johnson,** and **James Garfield.**

2. Who was the first president to appear on a postage stamp?

The first official U.S. government adhesive postage stamps were issued on July 1, 1847. **George Washington** appeared on the ten-cent denomination.

3. There have been six patches in American history when no former president was alive. Who was the first president to serve during years when no former president was alive?

[chuckle, chuckle; snort, snort] **George Washington.** There could be no former president alive during the term of our first president.

4. Who was the first vice president to become president?
John Adams. He succeeded **George Washington** as president.

5. Who was the first U.S. congressman to become president?
James Madison. Before he became our fourth president, he was the youngest member of the Continental Congress.

6. Who was the first president to wear trousers rather than knee breeches?
James Madison.

7. Who was the first wartime president?
James Madison. The War of 1812 raged during his administration. In that conflict, the British torched Washington, D.C.

8. Who was the first president to live in the White House when it was actually white?
James Monroe. When he began his presidency in 1817, the Executive Mansion was painted white. Before that, it was gray.

9. Who was the first president born outside of the original thirteen colonies?
Abraham Lincoln. He was born in Hodgenville, Kentucky.

10. Who was the first president to campaign actively?
William Henry Harrison. He was the first candidate to stump personally. His was the first campaign slogan: "Tippecanoe and Tyler, Too."

11. Who was the first vice president to assume the presidency because of the death of the president?

John Tyler. This happened as a result of the death of President **William Henry Harrison.**

12. Who was the first president to suffer the death of his wife while in office and the first to marry during his presidency?

John Tyler. His first wife, Letitia Christian, died while he was in office. He then married Julia Gardiner.

13. Who was the first president to be protected by a federally funded security force?

John Tyler. He was protected by a federally funded staff—of four.

14. Who was the first president for whom "Hail to the Chief" was played whenever he appeared?

John Tyler. The tradition of playing "Hail to the Chief" whenever a president appeared at a state function was started by his second wife, Julia Gardiner.

15. Who was the first president to be photographed while in office?

16. WHO WAS THE FIRST PRESIDENT TO WEAR A BEARD?

Abraham Lincoln. Some say he was simply responding to a letter from an eleven-year-old girl, Grace Bedell, who suggested that a beard would improve his appearance. **Benjamin Harrison** was the last bearded president and the mustachioed **William Howard Taft** the last to sport any facial hair. **William McKinley** was the only clean-shaven president between **Andrew Johnson** and **Woodrow Wilson.**

John Tyler. John Quincy Adams, Andrew Jackson, and Martin Van Buren were all photographed after serving their terms. During the brief month of William Henry Harrison's term, he was not in a condition to be photographed.

17. Who was the first "dark horse" candidate to become president?

James Polk. He was elected to the presidency in 1844. The other dark horse presidents were Franklin Pierce in 1852, Rutherford B. Hayes in 1876, James Garfield in 1880, and Warren G. Harding in 1920.

18. Who was the first president to retire voluntarily after his first term?

James Polk.

19. Who was the first president born in the nineteenth century?

Franklin Pierce. He entered the earthly stage in 1804.

20. Who was the first president whose party refused to nominate him for a second term?

Franklin Pierce. During Pierce's term as president, his own party adopted the campaign slogan "Anybody But Pierce." No surprise, then, that Pierce decided not to run for reelection. James Buchanan was nominated as an alternative to Pierce and won the endorsement on the seventeenth ballot.

21. Who was the first president to be assassinated?

Abraham Lincoln. Five days after the end of the Civil War, on April 5, 1865, Good Friday, he was fatally shot by the actor John Wilkes Booth. Three more presidents have been assassinated while in office—James Garfield, William McKinley, and John F. Kennedy.

22. WHO WAS THE FIRST PRESIDENT TO RIDE IN AN AUTOMOBILE?

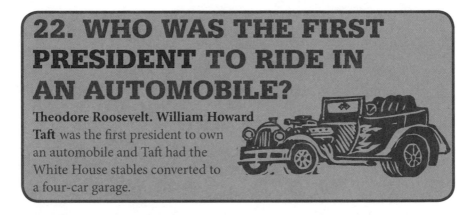

Theodore Roosevelt. William Howard Taft was the first president to own an automobile and Taft had the White House stables converted to a four-car garage.

23. Who was the first president to establish a national park?

Ulysses S. Grant. He established Yellowstone as the nation's first national park on March 1, 1872. In 1936, **Gerald Ford** served as a park ranger there, the only president who was employed by the National Park Service.

24. Who was the first president to have electric lights in the White House?

Benjamin Harrison. After he received an electric shock, his family was scared to death to use the light switches.

25. Who was the first president to attend a baseball game?

Benjamin Harrison. He saw the Cincinnati Reds beat the Washington Senators 7–4 on June 6, 1892.

26. Who was the first president to throw out "the first pitch"?

William Howard Taft. He started this tradition on April 4, 1910, during an opening day game between the Washington Senators and the Philadelphia Athletics. Since Taft's first pitch, every president but one, Jimmy Carter, has opened at least one baseball season during his tenure.

27. Who was the first president to officially refer to the Executive Mansion as the White House?

Theodore Roosevelt. He declared by presidential proclamation that the Executive Mansion should henceforth be known as "The White House" and was the first to use that term on presidential stationery.

28. Who was the first president to fly in an airplane?

Theodore Roosevelt. On October 11, 1910, he took a four-minute flight in a plane built by the Wright Brothers. The next Roosevelt—**Franklin D. Roosevelt**—was the first president to have a presidential aircraft.

29. Who was the first president to travel abroad during his term?

Theodore Roosevelt. He visited Panama in 1906 and was also the first president to visit every state. The first U.S. president to visit a European country while serving as president was **Woodrow Wilson,** who arrived at Brest, France, on December 13, 1918.

30. Who was the first president to win a Nobel Prize?

Theodore Roosevelt. He won the Nobel Peace Prize in 1906 for mediating the Russo-Japanese War Treaty. **Woodrow Wilson** and **Jimmy Carter** were also accorded that honor.

31. Who was the first president in whose election women were allowed to vote?

Warren G. Harding. This handsome man won an unprecedented 60 percent of the popular vote.

32. Who was the first sitting senator to be elected president?
Warren G. Harding. He was followed only by John F. Kennedy.

33. Who was the first vice president to become president and not seek a full second term?
Calvin Coolidge. Lyndon Johnson was the only other one to do so.

34. Who was the first president born west of the Mississippi River?
Herbert Hoover. His birthplace is the village of West Branch, Iowa.

35. Who was the first president whose mother was eligible to vote for him?
Franklin D. Roosevelt. His mother, Sara Ann Delano Roosevelt, was eligible to vote for him. By the way, she made him wear dresses for the first five years of his life.

36. Who was the first president to appoint a woman to his cabinet?
Franklin D. Roosevelt. Frances Perkins became the Secretary of Labor.

37. Under which president was the USO (United Services Organization) established?
Franklin D. Roosevelt. He approved the creation of the USO in 1941 as a private, nonprofit institution.

38. Which president began the tradition of the presidential library?
Franklin D. Roosevelt. He donated his papers to the United States in 1939 and asked the National Archives to administer them. His presidential library in Hyde Park, New York, was the first to be dedicated.

39. Who was the first president to assume office during wartime?
Harry S. Truman.

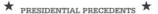

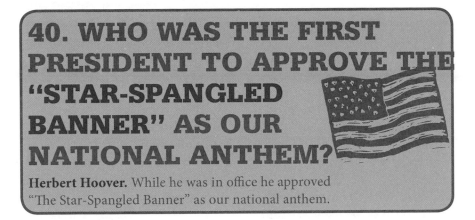

40. WHO WAS THE FIRST PRESIDENT TO APPROVE THE "STAR-SPANGLED BANNER" AS OUR NATIONAL ANTHEM?

Herbert Hoover. While he was in office he approved "The Star-Spangled Banner" as our national anthem.

41. Who was the first president of all fifty states?

Dwight Eisenhower. Hawaii became our fiftieth state on August 21, 1959, during the second half of his second term.

42. Who was the first president born in the twentieth century?

John F. Kennedy. He was born in Brookline, Massachusetts, on May 29, 1917. **Lyndon Johnson, Richard Nixon, Gerald Ford,** and **Ronald Reagan** were all born before JFK in the twentieth century but served after him.

43. Who was the first president to have served in the U.S. Navy?

John F. Kennedy. If the army was the most common branch of military service for earlier presidents, the navy attracted the greatest number of presidents who served in the second half of the twentieth century. JFK was followed by **Lyndon Johnson, Richard**

Nixon, Gerald Ford, Jimmy Carter, and **George H. W. Bush.**

44. Who was the first president to name an African American to his cabinet?
Lyndon Johnson. He chose Robert Weaver to head the new Department of Housing and Urban Development.

45. Who was the first president to visit all fifty states?
Richard Nixon.

46. Who was the first president to visit the Soviet Union and Mainland China?
Richard Nixon.

47. Who was the first president for whom eighteen-year-olds could vote?
Richard Nixon. The Twenty-Sixth Amendment to the Constitution was ratified by a majority of the states in 1971, during Richard Nixon's first term. It granted suffrage to eighteen-year-olds.

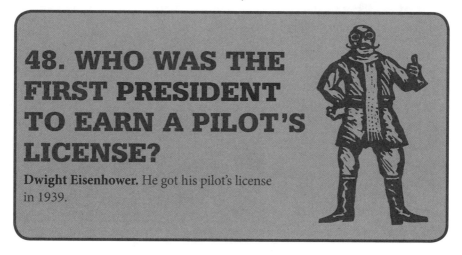

48. WHO WAS THE FIRST PRESIDENT TO EARN A PILOT'S LICENSE?

Dwight Eisenhower. He got his pilot's license in 1939.

49. Who was the first president born in a hospital?

Jimmy Carter. All previous presidents were born at home.

50. Who was the first baby boomer to be elected president?

Bill Clinton. Born August 19, 1946, he was the first baby boomer president and the first born after World War II. Born July 6, 1946, **George W. Bush** was the second presidential boomer.

CHAPTER II.
ONE AND ONLY PRESIDENTS

WHO WAS THE ONLY PRESIDENT WHO DID NOT SERVE IN WASHINGTON, D.C.?

George Washington. During his administration the nation's capital was located in Philadelphia.

It was **John Adams** who first occupied what was then known as The President's House, on 1600 Pennsylvania Avenue. The Adams family moved into the White House on November 1, 1800, while the paint was still drying. During the move, the family got lost for several hours in the woods north of Washington, D.C., Adams occupied The President's House for only four months, having lived most of his term in Philadelphia.

WHO WAS THE ONLY PRESIDENT TO BE UNANIMOUSLY ELECTED?

George Washington. He received all sixty-nine electoral votes from ten eligible states. In 1820, **James Monroe** received all the electoral votes except one. The single elector who voted against him was a New Hampshire delegate who felt strongly that only Washington should have the historical honor of being elected president unanimously.

Our first and fifth presidents are connected in other ways: George Washington (both terms) and James Monroe (second term) were the only two presidents to run unopposed. Washington and Monroe are also our only two presidents who had national capitals named after them —Washington, D.C., and Monrovia, the capital of Liberia.

Washington is the only president after whom a state is named, while four state capitals commemorate four other presidents—Jefferson City, Missouri; Madison, Wisconsin; Jackson, Mississippi; and Lincoln, Nebraska.

WHO WAS THE ONLY PRESIDENT TO RUN AS THE CANDIDATE OF A MAJOR PARTY IN A PRESIDENTIAL ELECTION AND COME OUT THIRD?

William Howard Taft. In 1912, he ran as a Republican for reelection against the Democratic nominee, **Woodrow Wilson. Theodore Roosevelt** said of Taft, "Taft meant well, but he meant well feebly," so Roosevelt also entered the presidential fray as a candidate for the Bull Moose party.

Roosevelt and Taft split the Republican vote, and Wilson won handily. Taft placed third with an abysmal 23 percent of the popular vote, the lowest ever for an incumbent president. Unremittingly good-humored, Taft sighed, "I have one consolation. No one candidate was ever elected ex-president by such a large majority."

Try your hand and brain at a quiz about presidential onlys. Again, the answers are mostly in the order of when each president served.

QUIZ

1. Who was the only president who did not represent a political party when he was first elected?
George Washington.

2. Who was the only president to attain the rank of six-star general?
George Washington. He commanded the Continental Army as a four-star general but was promoted posthumously to the position of six-star "General of the Armies of Congress"

by order of **Jimmy Carter,** who felt America's first president should also be America's highest military official.

3. Who were our only presidents to sign the Constitution?

George Washington and **James Madison.**

4. Who was the only president to be defeated by his vice president?

John Adams. He was defeated in 1801 by his vice president, **Thomas Jefferson,** the only president to experience that turnabout.

5. Who was the only president to found a university?

Thomas Jefferson. Our only red-headed president, Jefferson founded the University of Virginia in 1819. Before they became U.S. presidents, **James Garfield** was president of Hiram College, **Woodrow Wilson** was president of Princeton University, and **Dwight Eisenhower** was president of Columbia University.

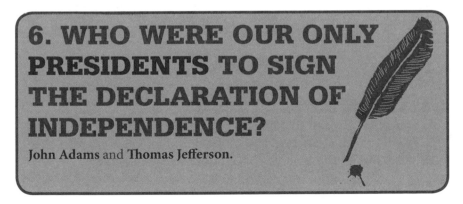

6. WHO WERE OUR ONLY PRESIDENTS TO SIGN THE DECLARATION OF INDEPENDENCE?

John Adams and Thomas Jefferson.

7. Who was the only president to have served in two different cabinet posts?
James Monroe. He served as Secretary of State and Secretary of War.

8. Who was the only president to serve in the House of Representatives after his presidency?
John Quincy Adams. He served in the House of Representatives for seventeen years and remains the only president to serve in the House after his presidential term ended. In 1848, he suffered a fatal cerebral stroke and fell to the floor of the House of Representatives. Missouri Senator Thomas Hart Benton eulogized, "Where else could death have found him but at the post of duty?"

9. Who was the only president to have served in both the American Revolution and the War of 1812?
Andrew Jackson. He was also the only president to have been a prisoner of war; he was captured during the Revolution at the age of thirteen.

10. Who was the only president to speak English as a second language?
Martin Van Buren. He was our first president of Dutch ancestry. He grew up speaking Dutch and his wife and he spoke Dutch at home.

11. Who was the only president who was the grandfather of another president?
William Henry Harrison. He was grandfather to Benjamin Harrison. The younger Harrison was named after his great-grandfather, a signer of the Declaration of Independence.

12. Who were the only two presidents who died in the White House itself?

William Henry Harrison (1841) and Zachary Taylor (1850).

13. Who was the only president to be named a sworn enemy of the United States?
John Tyler. He joined the Confederacy twenty years after he was in office and was declared a sworn enemy of the United States. He was also the only president who was not a U.S. citizen when he died; he died in Virginia as a citizen of the Confederate States of America. At his request, his coffin was draped with a Confederate flag.

14. Among presidents who served for at least one full term, who was the only one who had no turnover in his cabinet?
Franklin Pierce. There were no cabinet changes during the four years (1853–1857) of his presidency, the only time that has happened during a full presidential term.

15. Who was the only president to have been Speaker of the House of Representatives?
James Polk.

16. Who was the only president to be the father-in-law of another president?
Zachary Taylor. He was the father-in-law of Jefferson Davis, president of the Confederacy.

17. Who was the only president never to marry?
James Buchanan. He was known as the Bachelor President. During his term in office, his niece, Harriet Lane, assumed the role of First Lady. Previously in 1819, Buchanan had become engaged to Anne Coleman, daughter of the richest man in Pennsylvania. Through a misunderstanding their engagement was broken off. When Anne died mysteriously a short time later, Buchanan vowed he would never marry.

18. Who was the only president to be awarded a patent?

Abraham Lincoln. He was awarded a patent for a system of buoying vessels over shoals.

19. Who was the only president to serve in the Senate after his presidency?

Andrew Johnson. He is also the only former president elected to the U.S. Senate, the very body that almost kicked him out of office. His triumphant return to that body was short lived. In less than four months he died of a stroke.

20. Who was the only president to have been a preacher?

James Garfield.

21. Who was the only president to have personally hanged people?

Grover Cleveland. When he was sheriff of Erie County, New York, he placed the noose around the neck of two convicted criminals.

22. Who was the only president to be married in the White House?

Grover Cleveland. He entered the White House as a bachelor, but on June 2, 1886, at the age of forty-nine, he married twenty-one-year-old Frances Folsom in the Blue Room of the White House. Their baby, Ruth, was the first child born in the White House.

23. Who was the only president to serve two nonconsecutive terms?

Grover Cleveland. He was our twenty-second and twenty-fourth president, forever confusing the mathematics of the presidential sequence.

24. Who was the only president to serve as Supreme

Court Justice after his presidency?

William Howard Taft. He was appointed Chief Justice of the Supreme Court eight years after his presidency, the only man ever to have headed both the executive and judicial branches of our government.

25. Who is the only president buried in Washington, D.C.?

Woodrow Wilson. He is buried at the Washington National Cathedral. Wilson was also the only former president to retire to Washington, D.C.

26. Who were our only Quaker presidents?

Herbert Hoover and **Richard Nixon.** They were eighth cousins, once removed.

27. Who is the only president after whom two asteroids have been named?

Herbert Hoover. The asteroids Herberta and Hooveria were named in his honor. Less happily, the Hoovervilles (shantytowns of temporary dwellings that sprang up during the Great Depression) were also named for President Hoover, as were Hoover wagons (broken-down automobiles), Hoover blankets (newspapers used as blankets by the homeless), and Hoover flags (empty pockets turned inside out to show the penury of their owners). The asteroids Washingtonia, Quincy, Lincoln, and Grant have also been named for U.S. presidents.

28. Who was the only twentieth-century president who didn't attend college?

Harry S. Truman. There were nine presidents who never attended college, but Truman was the only one of them who served in the last century.

29. Who was the only bald president of the twentieth century?

Dwight Eisenhower. John Adams, John Quincy Adams, Martin Van Buren, and James Garfield were follicularly challenged among nineteenth-century presidents. Eisenhower is the only bald president elected during the twentieth century. More subjectively, among our presidents Andrew Jackson, John F. Kennedy, Ronald Reagan, and Bill Clinton had the best heads of hair.

30. Who was the only Roman Catholic president?

John F. Kennedy. Franklin D. Roosevelt spoke at the 1924 Democratic convention that nominated an earlier Catholic candidate for president, Al Smith.

31. Who was the only president to appoint his brother to a cabinet post?

John F. Kennedy. He appointed his brother, Robert F. Kennedy, to the post of Attorney General.

32. Who was the only president to be survived by both his parents?

John F. Kennedy. Assassinated at age forty-six, he is the only president whose parents both outlived him.

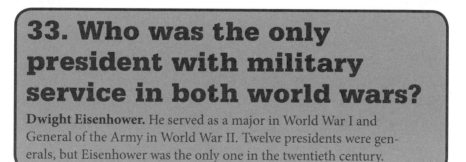

33. Who was the only president with military service in both world wars?

Dwight Eisenhower. He served as a major in World War I and General of the Army in World War II. Twelve presidents were generals, but Eisenhower was the only one in the twentieth century.

34. Who was the only president to be present at his predecessor's assassination?
Lyndon Johnson. He was in Dallas when **John F. Kennedy** was assassinated there.

35. Who was the only president to resign from office?
Richard Nixon. He resigned from the White House on August 9, 1974. Spiro Agnew, his vice president, had resigned earlier.

36. Who was the only man to be president and vice president but not elected to either office?
Gerald Ford. For two years, he was the only man who served as both vice president (replacing Agnew) and president (replacing Nixon) without having been elected to either office. The only elected office he ever held was a Western Michigan congressional seat. Ford's vice president, Nelson Rockefeller, was also never elected to his office. Ford also became the only president to pardon a former president.

37. Who was the only president to have become an Eagle Scout?
Gerald Ford.

38. Who was the only president who had had a career in modeling?
Gerald Ford. He appeared in a *Look* magazine pictorial and on the cover of *Cosmopolitan*.

39. Who was the only president to graduate from the U.S. Naval Academy?
Jimmy Carter. He graduated in the class of 1946. **Ulysses S. Grant** and **Dwight Eisenhower** were the only presidents to have graduated from West Point, the U.S. Military Academy.

40. Who was the only president to have been divorced?

Ronald Reagan. He had been married to actress Jane Wyman before marrying Nancy Davis, also an actress.

41. Who was the only president to have headed a labor union?

Ronald Reagan. He was president of the Screen Actors Guild.

42. Who was the only president to have been Director of the CIA?

George H. W. Bush.

43. Who was the only president to have been chairman of his political party?

George H. W. Bush.

44. Who was the only president to have been Ambassador to the United Nations?

George H. W. Bush.

45. Who was the only president to have been a Rhodes Scholar?

Bill Clinton. He graduated from Georgetown University in 1968 and won a Rhodes Scholarship to Oxford.

46. Who was the only Democratic president to win reelection during the second half of the twentieth century?

Bill Clinton. In 1996, he became the only Democratic president since Franklin D. Roosevelt to win reelection, a span of more than fifty years.

47. Who was the only president elected twice without receiving at least 50 percent of the popular vote either time?

Bill Clinton. He received 43 percent of the popular vote in 1992 and 49 percent in 1996.

48. Who was the only president to have earned an MBA (Master of Business Administration)?

George W. Bush. He earned an MBA from the Harvard Business School, the only president with that degree.

49. Who was the only president to have been an owner of a major league baseball team?

George W. Bush. He was the only managing general partner of a major league baseball team (the Texas Rangers) to become president.

50. WHO WAS THE ONLY PRESIDENT TO HAVE OFFICIALLY REPORTED A UFO SIGHTING?

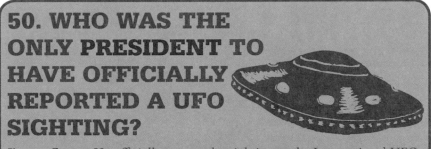

Jimmy Carter. He officially reported a sighting to the International UFO Bureau. He described a noiseless object "as bright as the moon" that came within 900 yards of his party.

CHAPTER III.
PRESIDENTIAL
RECORD SETTERS

CAN YOU NAME THE YOUNGEST MAN EVER TO HAVE SERVED AS PRESIDENT OF THE UNITED STATES?

If your answer is **John F. Kennedy,** you're not quite correct. Kennedy was, at the age of forty-three years and seven months, the youngest man ever to have been elected president, but **Theodore Roosevelt** became president at the age of forty-two years and ten months, when **William McKinley** was assassinated. When TR's second term was over, he was still only fifty years old, making him the youngest ex-president.

WHICH OF OUR PRESIDENTS APPOINTED THE GREATEST NUMBER OF SUPREME COURT JUSTICES?

The answer—of course—is **George Washington.** [Chuckle chuckle, snort snort again.] During his two terms he appointed eleven Justices. The number of Supreme Court Justices has changed over the years, ranging from six at the outset to ten. President **Franklin D. Roosevelt** tried to increase the court to fifteen members, but the number has remained nine since 1869.

Now cast your ballot for a quiz about presidential mosts:

QUIZ

1. Now that you know the identity of our youngest president, who was our oldest president?

Ronald Reagan. He became president at sixty-nine, older than anyone else, and left office a few months shy of his seventy-eighth birthday. Before Reagan, **Dwight Eisenhower** had been the only president to reach the age of seventy while in office. **William Henry Harrison** attained the office at the age of sixty-eight but died only a month later. The average age at which America's presidents have taken office is fifty-four.

2. Which president lived the longest?

Gerald Ford. When **Ronald Reagan** died at the age of ninety-three years and a hundred and twenty days, he was our longest-lived president. But, on November 12, 2006, Ford surpassed that record and lived another month and a half past that age. Amazingly, our third longest-lived president is **John Adams,** who was born in 1735 and who lived for ninety years and eight months, followed by **Herbert Hoover,** at ninety years and two months.

3. Which man spent the greatest number of years as a former president?

Herbert Hoover. He was a former president the longest—thirty-one years, seven months, and seventeen days.

4. Which president spent the shortest period as a former president?

James Polk. He once proclaimed, "No president who performs his duties faithfully and conscientiously can have any leisure." He meant it: during Polk's four years in office, his wife Sara and he spent only six weeks away from the job. Over that span, no dancing, singing, or alcohol was permitted in the White House. He died just three months into his retirement, quite possibly from exhaustion.

5. WHO WAS OUR FATTEST PRESIDENT?

William Howard Taft. At 6 feet 2 inches and weighing 300 to 340 pounds, he was our fullest-figured president. After he became stuck in the White House bathtub, Taft ordered a new one installed that would accommodate four men of average stature. Although Taft was the most portly president, he was considered a good dancer, a good tennis player, and a decent golfer.

Grover Cleveland, at 5 feet 10 inches and 260 pounds, held the weighty record before Taft. Cleveland, sometimes called "the buxom Buffalonian," confessed that he was helpless in the presence of sausage, corned beef and cabbage, and thick-foamed German beer.

6. Which president lived the shortest length of time?

John F. Kennedy. He took office at the age of forty-three, and after two-and-a-half years (exactly a thousand days), he was assassinated at the age of forty-six. **James Polk** was our shortest-lived president to die out of office, at age fifty-three.

7. Who was our tallest president?

Abraham Lincoln. At 6 feet 3¾ inches, Lincoln was our loftiest president. To the inevitable question "How tall are you?" Lincoln would reply, "Tall enough to reach the ground." **Lyndon Johnson** reached the second-greatest height at 6 feet 3½ inches. **George Washington** and **Thomas Jefferson** measured up in third place at 6 feet 2½ inches. Like our population, the average height of presidents has grown taller and is currently 5 feet 10 inches, although some of our tallest presidents came early. Our tallest First Lady was Eleanor Roosevelt at 6 feet; her husband was 6 feet 2 inches. Almost all our presidents were taller than the average American living contemporaneously and taller than their closest opponent.

8. Who was our shortest president?

James Madison. At 5 feet 3¾ inches and weighing about a hundred pounds, he was our most compact president. The author Washington Irving described him as "but a withered little apple-John." **Martin Van Buren** and **Benjamin Harrison** towered over Madison at 5 feet 6 inches.

9. Which president had the biggest feet?

Warren G. Harding. He had the largest feet, size 14. **George Washington, Abraham Lincoln,** and **Bill Clinton** each wore a size 13 boot and shoe.

10. Who was president for the shortest period of time?

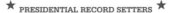

William Henry Harrison. He died on the thirty-first day of his presidency. As a result, 1841 was a year in which three American presidents served—**Martin Van Buren,** Harrison, and **John Tyler.** Forty years later, in 1881, **Rutherford B. Hayes, James Garfield** (assassinated), and **Chester A. Arthur** served.

11. Who was president for the longest period of time?

Franklin D. Roosevelt. He was elected to four terms as president and served from 1933 to 1945. This record can't be broken as long as the Twenty-Second Amendment, setting a limit of two terms, remains in effect. The exact wording is: "No person shall be elected to the office of the President more than twice, and no person who has held the office of President, or acted as President, for more than two years of a term to which some other person was elected President shall be elected to the office of the President more than once."

12. Which president had the greatest number of children?

John Tyler. He had three sons and five daughters with his first wife and five sons and two daughters with his second, for a total of fifteen offspring. From a single marriage **William Henry Harrison** was the father of ten children—four girls and six boys, one of whom became the father of another president, **Benjamin Harrison.** Hence, the Harrison-Tyler ticket of 1840 was the most prolific in American history, producing a total of twenty-five children.

13. Which president was our most devoted reader of the Bible?

John Quincy Adams. He read the Bible cover to cover every year.

14. Which president ran in the greatest number of presidential and vice presidential elections as a Republican?

Richard M. Nixon. He ran successfully as a Republican candidate for the office of vice president in 1952 and 1956, unsuccessfully for president in 1960, and successfully for president in 1968 and 1972. Total: five.

15. Which president ran in the greatest number of presidential and vice presidential elections as a Democrat?
Franklin D. Roosevelt. He ran unsuccessfully as a Democratic candidate

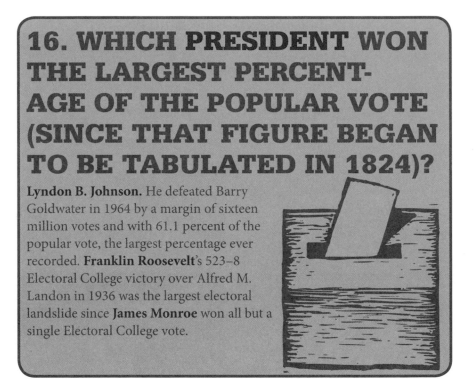

16. WHICH PRESIDENT WON THE LARGEST PERCENTAGE OF THE POPULAR VOTE (SINCE THAT FIGURE BEGAN TO BE TABULATED IN 1824)?

Lyndon B. Johnson. He defeated Barry Goldwater in 1964 by a margin of sixteen million votes and with 61.1 percent of the popular vote, the largest percentage ever recorded. **Franklin Roosevelt**'s 523–8 Electoral College victory over Alfred M. Landon in 1936 was the largest electoral landslide since **James Monroe** won all but a single Electoral College vote.

for the office of vice president in 1920 and successfully for president in 1932, 1936, 1940, and 1944. Total: five.

17. Who was our most traveled president?

Bill Clinton. He set a record for the most trips abroad: 133.

18. Which president pardoned the greatest number of people?

Andrew Johnson. He granted a pardon on May 29, 1865, to all former confederates who promised to support the Union and obey the laws against slavery.

19. Which president served the shortest full single term?

John Adams. From John Adams to **George H. W. Bush,** eleven presidents have served a full single term. Ten of them served for 1,461 days, but John Adams served for only 1,460 because there was no Leap Year during his span.

20. Who was our most athletic president?

Gerald Ford. This is, of course, a matter of opinion, but he was a star center on the University of Michigan football team. In his *Saturday Night Live* skits, comedian Chevy Chase created an image of Ford as a bumbling stumbler. But consider the facts: Ford turned down offers to play professionally for the Chicago Bears and the Green Bay Packers. He was head boxing coach and assistant football coach at Yale University. He was an above-average tennis player, and he scored a hole in one in the Memphis Open.

CHAPTER IV.
PATTERNS OF THE
PRESIDENCY

WHICH TWO PRESIDENTS DIED ON THE VERY SAME DAY?

John Adams and **Thomas Jefferson.** Our second and third presidents were political rivals, then friends; both died on July 4, 1826, exactly fifty years after the signing of the Declaration of Independence.

As Jefferson lay weak and dying at his home Monticello on the evening of July 3, he whispered, "Is this the Fourth?" To quiet the former president, his young lawyer friend Nicholas Trist answered, "Yes." Jefferson fell asleep with a smile on his face. His heart continued to beat until the next day, July Fourth, when the bells rang out and the fireworks exploded in celebration of the signing of the Declaration of Independence.

At dawn of that same day, Adams was expiring in his home in Quincy, Massachusetts. A servant asked the fading Adams, "Do you know what day it is?" "Oh yes," responded the lion in winter. "It is the glorious Fourth of July." He then lapsed into a stupor but awakened in the afternoon and sighed feebly, "Thomas Jefferson survives." He ceased to breathe around sunset, about six hours after Jefferson.

James Monroe also died on July 4, five years later, and **Calvin Coolidge** was born on July 4, 1872. **James Madison** was offered drugs so that he might live until July 4 but refused them and expired on June 28, 1836.

The more we delve into the lives of our American presidents, the more we see patterns that connect their feats, their fates, their families, and their foibles:

- The ancestry of all forty-two presidents through George W. Bush has been limited to the following seven heritages, or some combination thereof: Dutch, English, German, Irish, Scottish, Swiss, and Welsh. The most common religious affiliation has been Episcopalian, the second most common Presbyterian.

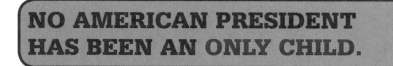

NO AMERICAN PRESIDENT HAS BEEN AN ONLY CHILD.

- More than half our presidents (twenty-two) have served as governors, the first being **Thomas Jefferson** (Virginia) and the most recent **George W. Bush** (Texas).

- More than a third of our presidents (fifteen) have been U.S. senators, the first being **James Monroe** (Virginia) and the most recent **Richard Nixon** (California).

- More than half of our presidents (twenty-two) have been lawyers, the first being **John Adams** and the most recent **Bill Clinton.**

- No American president has been an only child. All have had at least one full sibling, except for **Franklin D. Roosevelt, Gerald Ford,** and **Bill Clinton,** who grew up with half siblings. Twenty-three of our presidents have been first-born males, while six have been the youngest child in their family.

- Six of the forty-two men who served as president had no children, the last one being Warren G. Harding, who married a divorcée five years his senior in 1891. The marriage lasted thirty-two years but produced no offspring. The other childless presidents were James Buchanan, James Polk, Andrew Jackson, James Madison, and George Washington. That Washington was childless helped ensure that the presidency would not become a blood-heir monarchy.

- Virginia is the birth state of the greatest number of our presidents, including seven of the first twelve: **George Washington, Thomas Jefferson, James Madison, James Monroe, William Henry Harrison, John Tyler**, and **Zachary Taylor**, as well as **Woodrow Wilson**.

- Ohio is known as the "Mother of Presidents" because eight American presidents came from Ohio: **William Henry Harrison, Ulysses S. Grant, Rutherford B. Hayes, James Garfield** (that's three in a row), **Benjamin Harrison, William McKinley, William Howard Taft**, and **Warren G. Harding**.

- Harvard boasts the most presidents as alumni (six in all): **John Adams, John Quincy Adams, Theodore Roosevelt, Franklin Roosevelt, John Kennedy**, and **George W. Bush** (business school). Yale is a close second, with five presidents as alumni: **William Howard Taft, Gerald Ford** (law school), **George H. W. Bush, Bill Clinton** (law school), and **George W. Bush**.

- Presidents' Day is the official designation of a federal holiday that is now celebrated on the third Monday of February. The original celebration was in honor of **George Washington**, whose actual birthday was February 22. **Abraham Lincoln,** who was born February 12, was added to the mix, and in the late 1980s, Presidents' Day (note the apostrophe *after* the *s* to indicate that more than *one* president is being celebrated) became the official designation. Our American presidents have influenced other holidays:

  ★ **Rutherford B. Hayes** and his wife Lucy conducted the first Easter egg roll on the White House lawn.

  ★ On November 26, 1789, **George Washington** established the first national celebration of Thanksgiving. In 1863, **Abraham Lincoln,** hoping to unite a sundered nation, issued a proclamation declaring Thanksgiving a national holiday to be celebrated on the last Thursday of November. He did this

FRANKLIN D. ROOSEVELT MOVED TURKEY DAY UP TO GIVE AMERICANS MORE TIME FOR CHRISTMAS SHOPPING.

at the urging of Sarah Josepha Hale, the poet and editor who wrote the children's rhyme "Mary Had a Little Lamb." **Franklin D. Roosevelt** moved turkey day up a week to the third Thursday in November to give Americans more time for Christmas shopping. Controversy followed, and Congress passed a joint resolution in 1941 decreeing that Thanksgiving should fall on the fourth Thursday of each November, where it remains. **Harry S. Truman** established the tradition of granting a presidential pardon to a Thanksgiving turkey, who is then retired—alive and gobbling— to a petting farm.

★ Placing a decorated Christmas tree in the White House began in 1889 on Christmas morning during the presidency of **Benjamin Harrison.** In 1913, **Woodrow Wilson** asked for a community Christmas tree to be placed at the Capitol so that a tree-lighting ceremony could be recognized as a national event.

- Four pairs of presidents defeated each other in successive elections: **John Adams** won over **Thomas Jefferson** in 1796; Jefferson defeated Adams in 1800; **John Quincy Adams** was elected over **Andrew Jackson** in 1824; Jackson beat Adams in 1828; **Martin Van Buren** defeated **William Henry Harrison** in 1836; Harrison outpolled Van Buren in 1840; **Benjamin Harrison** edged **Grover Cleveland** in 1888; Cleveland defeated Harrison in 1892.

- Four Presidents won the presidency but lost the popular vote: **Andrew Jackson** won the popular vote but lost the election to **John Quincy Adams** (1824); Samuel J. Tilden won the popular vote but lost the election to

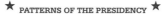

Rutherford B. Hayes (1876); **Grover Cleveland** won the popular vote but lost the election to **Benjamin Harrison** (1888); Al Gore won the popular vote but lost the election to **George W. Bush** (2000).

- Only thirteen (less than a third) of our forty-two presidents have served at least two terms, including five of the first seven who occupied the office and three of the last four.

- **John Adams** and **John Quincy Adams** are the only two presidents among our first seven to leave office after a single term.

- Two of our chief executives apparently forgot that they were presidents:

  ★ **Thomas Jefferson** left specific instructions for the message to be carved on his tombstone:

  > *Here was buried Thomas Jefferson,*
  > *Author of the Declaration of Independence*
  > *Of the Statute of Virginia for Religious Freedom*
  > *A Father of the University of Virginia*

  Do you see what's missing? Apparently, Jefferson didn't think it important enough to include his two terms as President of the United States.

  ★ **William Howard Taft**'s lifelong ambition was to be Chief Justice of the Supreme Court, and he was appointed to that position by **Warren G.**

Harding eight years after his presidency. So rewarding was this turn of events that he later said, "I don't remember that I was ever president."

> # JOHN QUINCY ADAMS NAMED HIS ELDEST SON GEORGE WASHINGTON.

- **Martin Van Buren** was the eighth president and the eighth vice president. He lived to see the election of eight different presidents from eight different states.

- Seven presidents elected at intervals of twenty years died in office—**William Henry Harrison** (elected in 1840), **Abraham Lincoln** (1860) **James Garfield** (1880), **William McKinley** (1900), **Warren G. Harding** (1920), **Franklin D. Roosevelt** (1940), and **John F. Kennedy** (1960). First noted in a Ripley's *Believe It or Not* book published in 1934, this string of untimely presidential deaths is known variously as the curse of Tippecanoe, the zero-year curse, the twenty-year curse, and Tecumseh's curse (Tecumseh being the chief defeated by **William Henry Harrison** at the battle of Tippecanoe in 1811). **Ronald Reagan**, elected in 1980 and shot by John Hinckley Jr., almost continued the deadly sequence but survived and broke the curse.

- The challenges to the health of our presidents could be collected into an encyclopedia of medical maladies and mishaps. Here are a few of the most famous and bizarre:

  ★ **George Washington** suffered severe tooth loss that made it difficult for him to eat and even speak. He began developing severe dental problems from cracking walnuts with his teeth. At his inauguration, Washington had but a single tooth. At various times he wore dentures made of human or animal teeth, ivory, or lead—never wood. Wooden teeth would have filled Washington's maw full of rotting pulp. Washington's lack of teeth altered the shape of his once-handsome face, resulting in the famous pinched look in his later portraits. Because Martha Washington had delivered four children during her previous marriage, it appears that Washington's infertility was the reason that the Father of Our Country never became a father.

  ★ A contemporary reporter described **Abraham Lincoln** thusly: "a tall, lank, lean man considerably over six feet in height with long, pendulous arms terminating in hands of extraordinary dimension which, however, were far exceeded in proportion by his feet." Lincoln's physical dimensions have led many a medical detective to conjecture that he was a victim of Marfan syndrome, a connective tissue disorder.

  ★ **Ulysses S. Grant** claimed to smoke seven to ten cigars a day. When word got out of Grant's love of stogies, people sent him more than 10,000 boxes of cigars. He died of throat cancer.

★ In 1893, at the start of his second term, **Grover Cleveland** was diagnosed with cancer and secretly underwent an operation to have a portion of his left jaw replaced with a rubber substitute. The surgery was conducted on the presidential yacht and was not disclosed to the press or even the vice president until after Cleveland's presidency.

★ Perhaps because of chronic depression, **Calvin Coolidge** slept eleven hours a day and always took an afternoon nap lasting at least two hours. Social observer H. L. Mencken wrote of Coolidge, "His chief feat during five years and seven months in office was to sleep more than any other President—to sleep more and say less." At a performance of the Marx Brothers show *Animal Crackers*, Groucho Marx discovered Coolidge in the audience and cried out to him. "Isn't it past your bedtime, Cal?" The president laughed heartily, along with the audience. When *New Yorker* writer and wit Dorothy Parker was informed that Coolidge had died, she asked, "How can they tell?"

AT HARVARD, THEODORE ROOSEVELT ALMOST WON THE LIGHTWEIGHT BOXING CHAMPIONSHIP.

While boxing in the White House with heavyweight champion John L. Sullivan, Roosevelt received a blow to his face that left him blind in his left eye. He was so nearsighted in the other eye that he always carried a dozen pairs of glasses with him in case he needed a replacement.

FROM ABRAHAM LINCOLN TO BENJAMIN HARRISON, EVERY PRESIDENT TO HAVE A BEARD HAS BEEN A REPUBLICAN.

★ At the age of thirty-nine, **Franklin D. Roosevelt** was paralyzed by polio. He served his entire presidency without the use of his legs but, through rigorous exercise, learned to stand with the help of braces. His wheelchair was designed with no arms to give the appearance of a regular chair. Roosevelt seldom mentioned his polio but once observed, "If you had spent two years in bed trying to wiggle your big toe, after that anything else would seem easy."

★ **John F. Kennedy** may well have been the worst medical mess ever to occupy the White House. His maladies—colitis, steroid complications, chronic back pain, and Addison's disease with resulting chronic fatigue, to name just a few—were kept from the public eye before Kennedy's election and during his service as president.

• Thirty of our forty-two presidents have served in the military. (All presidents have been Commander-in-Chief, but that does not strictly count as military service.)

- **John Tyler** was born when **George Washington** was president. His youngest daughter, Mary—born when Tyler was seventy years of age—died during the administration of Harry S. Truman. That's a span of thirty-two presidents—more than a hundred and fifty years.

- Seven presidents have had their names legally changed. You can recognize the first five from their birth-certificate names—Hiram Ulysses Grant, Stephen Grover Cleveland, Thomas Woodrow Wilson, John Calvin Coolidge, and David Dwight Eisenhower. As for the last two: Gerald Ford, born Leslie Lynch King Jr., was renamed after his adoptive father, and **William Jefferson Clinton** was born William Jefferson Blythe IV three months after his father died in an automobile accident. When his mother wed Roger Clinton, he took the family name.

- **George Washington** (in his younger days), **Warren G. Harding, John F. Kennedy**, and **Ronald Reagan** are generally ranked as our handsomest presidents. At least two other presidents have been able to joke about their unbecoming looks:

  ★**Abraham Lincoln** was known to make fun of his legendary homeliness and gangly height. During one of their debates, Stephen Douglas accused Lincoln of being two-faced. Replied Lincoln calmly, "I leave it to my audience: If I had two faces, would I be wearing this one?" Lincoln was frequently compared to a monkey, an ape, and an "ape baboon," if such a thing is possible. One wonders if that had anything to do with the happenstance that Lincoln and Charles Darwin were both born on February 12, 1809. When a grouchy old Democrat said to him,

ABRAHAM LINCOLN WAS KNOWN TO MAKE FUN OF HIS LEGENDARY HOMELINESS AND GANGLY HEIGHT.

"They say you are a self-made man," Lincoln riposted, "Well, all I've got to say is that it was a damned bad job."

★ **Woodrow Wilson** composed a limerick to describe his horsy visage:

> *For beauty I am not a star.*
> *There are others more handsome by far.*
> *But my face, I don't mind it*
> *Because I'm behind it.*
> *It's the people in front whom I jar.*

- **James Garfield** entertained friends by writing Latin with one hand and Greek with the other. He was primarily left-handed, along with presidents **Harry S. Truman, Gerald Ford, George H. W. Bush,** and **Bill Clinton**. Clinton was the only left-handed president elected to two terms.

- During their terms of service, all but two of our presidents—**Millard Fillmore** and **Chester Arthur**—had pets. Two of our chief executives were stunningly imaginative (dare we say compulsive?) animal collectors:

  ★ During his presidency, **Theodore Roosevelt** owned six dogs, two cats, a gray squirrel, a pony, a pig, a badger, a garter snake, a piebald rat, four Guinea pigs, a hen, a macaw, and a one-legged rooster.

  ★ **Calvin Coolidge** owned six dogs, a cat (which would cleave to his clothing as he walked around the White House), two raccoons, a donkey, a

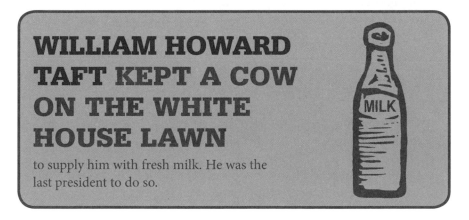

WILLIAM HOWARD TAFT KEPT A COW ON THE WHITE HOUSE LAWN

to supply him with fresh milk. He was the last president to do so.

goose, a bobcat, a wallaby, two lion cubs, an antelope, and a pygmy hippo during his presidency.

- Two other twentieth-century presidents kept farm animals outside the White House:

  ★ During **Woodrow Wilson**'s presidency, his wife introduced a flock of sheep to graze on the White House lawn. Their wool was sold to raise money for the Red Cross during World War I. One newspaper inadvertently left out the word *sheep* when it wrote, "Woodrow Wilson's wife grazed on the front lawn of the White House."

- Three U.S. presidents have been the sons of clergymen—**Chester A. Arthur, Grover Cleveland**, and **Woodrow Wilson**.

- **William McKinley** was the last president to have fought in the Civil War. **Ulysses S. Grant, Rutherford B. Hayes, James A. Garfield**, and **Benjamin Harrison** also fought in the Civil War.

- Both **Theodore Roosevelt** and **Franklin D. Roosevelt** served as governor of New York and as Assistant Secretary of the Navy.

- At least two of our presidents have had something to say about the art and science of spelling:

  ★ **Andrew Jackson,** whom some accused of being illiterate, observed, "It's a damn small mind that can think of only one way to spell a word."

WILLIAM MCKINLEY WAS THE LAST PRESIDENT TO HAVE FOUGHT IN THE CIVIL WAR.

★ **Theodore Roosevelt** was an enthusiastic champion of simplified spelling. In 1906, he sent his annual message to Congress in simplified spelling. "Nothing escapes Mr. Roosevelt," wrote the *Louisville Courier-Journal*. "No subject is tu hi fr him to takl, nor tu lo for him tu notis."

• **George Washington, John Adams,** and **Thomas Jefferson** were all avid collectors and players of marbles. **John Tyler** was playing marbles when he learned that he had become president. But golf is the sport most associated with American presidents:

★ **William Howard Taft** was the first president to take up the game.

★ **Woodrow Wilson** was adamant about playing golf year-round and any time of day. He used red balls for snow days and had his caddie tote a large flashlight for play at night. One particular match didn't end until five o'clock in the morning. Wilson claimed that golf was a game of amusement, not competition, and seldom kept score. On several occasions his wife Edith joined him on the links, a rarity for a woman, let alone a First Lady.

★ The most notable golfer among presidents, **Dwight Eisenhower** played golf as many as a hundred and fifty days a year, often walked the halls with a pitching wedge, and had a putting green installed on the White House lawn. Located at the seventeenth hole at Augusta National Golf Club is a loblolly pine officially called the "Eisenhower Tree." The former president and club member hit into the tree so often he campaigned to have it cut down, a proposal rejected by the club's board of governors. The pine has been linked to Eisenhower ever since. When Ike ran for reelection in 1956, there were bumper stickers that quipped, "Ben Hogan for president. If we're going to have a golfer—let's have a good one!"

★ Despite a bad back and lack of practice, **John F. Kennedy** often shot in the mid to high seventies.

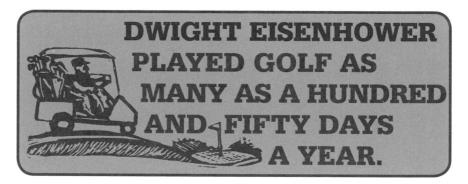

★ **Richard Nixon** scored a hole in one on Labor Day 1961 at the Bel Air Country Club in Los Angeles. **Dwight Eisenhower** aced the par-three thirteenth hole at Seven Lakes Country Club.

★ **Gerald Ford** hit many a stellar golf shot in pro-am tournaments (and a hole in one in the Memphis Open), but he became best known for peppering galleries with wild hooks and topped liners that occasionally met somebody's limb or head. Ford was often paired with comedian Bob Hope, who stoked the president's reputation when he called him "the man who made golf a contact sport" and "the most dangerous driver since Ben-Hur." Hope once zinged, "It's not hard to find Jerry Ford on a golf course—you just follow the wounded." On another occasion Hope quipped, "Whenever I play with him, I usually try to make it a foursome—the president, myself, a paramedic, and a faith healer." He added, "I'm comfortable playing with [Ford] as long as my caddie and I have the same blood type."

★ **George H. W. Bush** and **George W. Bush** come from a prominent golfing family that includes H. W.'s grandfather, George Herbert Walker, founder of the Walker Cup tournament, and H. W.'s father Prescott Bush, who served as head of the USGA.

• **William Howard Taft** and **John F. Kennedy** are the only two presidents to be buried in Arlington National Cemetery.

- Since the start of the twentieth century, only three men have become president without having held major elective office—**William Howard Taft, Herbert Hoover**, and **Dwight Eisenhower**.

- **Theodore Roosevelt** and **Ronald Reagan** were each responsible for the success of two major commercial products:

  ⋆ Early in 1903, a stuffed animal then known as "teddy's bear" began to gain what would become enormous and enduring popularity. The manufacturers, Rose and Morris Michtom, who ran a novelty store in Brooklyn, claimed that they received permission from **Theodore Roosevelt** to create and distribute the toy. Roosevelt used the bear as a symbol in his successful 1904 presidential election. Now, more than a century later, children still hug their adorable teddy bears.

  ⋆ **Theodore Roosevelt** was prone to asthma attacks as a child and, on doctor's orders, began drinking coffee to arrest these onslaughts. Over time, he grew to love coffee. In 1907, the president took a drink of coffee at an exhibition booth and, when offered a second cup, he exclaimed, "Delighted! It's good to the last drop!" Maxwell House brand coffee took their motto from that exclamation, and it remains theirs even to this day, a century later.

  ⋆ **Ronald Reagan** generated booming sales of two products: hearing aids, because he used one, and jelly beans, because he told reporters he liked them.

- Given the high-stakes gamble of being president, it's no surprise that five of our twentieth century presidents have played the game of poker:

  ★ The first president who we are sure played poker was **Grover Cleveland.** He was an especially hard-working president and took time off on many a Sunday afternoon to play the game. "My father used to say that it was wicked to go fishing on Sunday," he once explained, "but he never said anything about draw-poker."

  ★ **Warren G. Harding**'s advisers were known as the Poker Cabinet because they frequently played poker together while liquor flowed freely despite Prohibition. Harding played at least twice a week and once gambled away a priceless set of White House china dating back to the administration of **Rutherford B. Hayes.**

  ★ Because of paraplegia brought on by his polio, **Franklin D. Roosevelt** was unable to relax by taking long walks or playing golf or tennis. But

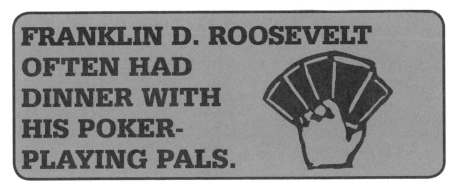

FRANKLIN D. ROOSEVELT OFTEN HAD DINNER WITH HIS POKER-PLAYING PALS.

he often had dinner with his poker-playing pals and then adjourned to a marathon session of cards. His favorite game was seven-card stud. Among the regulars were the Vice President, Speaker of the House, Attorney General, Secretary of Commerce, and at least one Supreme Court Justice. The President's secretary, "Missy" LeHand, served cocktails and often played in the game. One of the rules was that nobody could discuss anything serious at the evening poker sessions. The only thought was how to outfox the other players.

★ Roosevelt selected as his last vice president another poker player. **Harry S. Truman** was playing poker when he found out that he had become president. Truman was known as an excellent poker player, and "The buck stops here" became the famous slogan of his administration. (The "buck" actually refers to a betting marker in poker.) In office for just a few months, Truman had to decide whether or not to drop the atomic bomb on Japanese cities in order to bring World War II to a close. To help him focus during the decision-making process, Truman engaged in an almost continuous game of pot-limit poker aboard the presidential yacht, the *Williamsburg*. Often all three branches of government were represented at the poker table. The group would board the ship Friday afternoon and sail the Potomac until Sunday afternoon.

★ Born a Quaker, **Richard Nixon** remained unfamiliar with any form of gambling until his mid-twenties. But during his World War II years in the Navy, Nixon won $6,000, which helped to fund his initial—and successful—run for Congress.

HERBERT HOOVER DONATED HIS ENTIRE PRESIDENTIAL SALARY TO CHARITY.

- **Franklin D. Roosevelt** was a fifth cousin of **Theodore Roosevelt**, a fifth cousin once removed of his wife, Eleanor Roosevelt, and a seventh cousin once removed of Winston Churchill. Genealogists have determined that FDR was related to eleven other presidents: **George Washington, John Adams, James Madison, John Quincy Adams, Martin Van Buren, William Henry Harrison, Zachary Taylor, Ulysses S. Grant, Benjamin Harrison, Theodore Roosevelt**, and **William Howard Taft**.

- A temperance committee visited **Abraham Lincoln** and asked him to fire General **Ulysses S. Grant.** Surprised, Lincoln asked why. "He drinks too much," answered the spokesman for the group. "Well," said Lincoln. "I wish some of you would tell me the brand of whiskey that Grant drinks. I would like to send a barrel of it to every one of my other generals."

- The first time that conservative standard bearer **Ronald Reagan** voted for a president, he cast his ballot for New Dealer **Franklin D. Roosevelt.**

- Because of the Watergate scandals, many people accuse **Richard Nixon** of having been the most nefarious president in our history. Not so in 1960, the year in which Nixon lost an extremely close presidential election to **John F. Kennedy.** Accusations of voting fraud flew, and Nixon was encouraged to protest the result. But he stepped aside, explaining, "If I were to demand a recount, the organization of the new administration and the orderly transfer of responsibility from the old to the new might be delayed for months. The situation within the entire federal government would be chaotic." Years later, Nixon's successor, **Gerald Ford,** would use the same logic when he pardoned Nixon of all crimes.

- One of our most intelligent presidents, **Jimmy Carter** could speed-read two thousand words per minute. Carter and **Herbert Hoover** were our only two presidents who were engineers. **John F. Kennedy** constantly astounded all those around him with his knowledge of current events. It is said that he could read four newspapers in twenty minutes.

- **George H. W. Bush** was the first president born in June. Before Bush, presidents had been born during the other eleven months.

- As a delegate to Boys Nation while in high school, **Bill Clinton** met President **John F. Kennedy** in the White House Rose Garden in 1962. The encounter led him to enter a life of public service. Years earlier, **Franklin D. Roosevelt**'s parents visited their friend, President **Grover Cleveland**. In the White House, Cleveland looked little five-year-old Franklin in the eye and wearily declared, "My little man, I am making a strange wish for you, a wish I suppose no one else could make. It is my wish you never be the president of the United States." Roosevelt grew up to become the only president who served four terms.

- Formerly bitter political rivals **George H. W. Bush** and **Bill Clinton** joined forces to raise funds for victims of the Indian Ocean tsunami in 2004 and Hurricane Katrina in 2005.

- **George Washington**'s salary as president was $25,000, **George W. Bush**'s $400,000. But Washington's would be worth about $531,000 today.

- Despite an inclination for presidents to bloviate, at least two of our chief executives have praised the value of speaking briefly and to the point:

  ★ Once a Cabinet member praised **Woodrow Wilson** for his short speeches and asked him how long it took him to prepare them. "It depends," Wilson told him. "If I am to speak ten minutes, I need a week for preparation; if fifteen minutes, three days; if half an hour, two days; if an hour, I am ready now."

  ★ **Franklin D. Roosevelt,** one of the finest speakers to be president, had this advice about the art of public speaking: "Be sincere; be brief; be seated."

CHAPTER V.
PRESIDENTS UNDER FIRE

THE ORIGINAL ASSASSINS were a militant branch of Shiite Muslims who opposed the rule of Sunni caliphs from the eighth to the fourteenth centuries. The word *assassin* was derived from *hassasin*, "hashish user," because it was thought that these militants ingested hashish to inspire them to commit political murder.

Four presidents have died from assassins' bullets—**Abraham Lincoln** in 1865, **James Garfield** in 1881, **William McKinley** in 1901, and **John F. Kennedy** in 1963.

- On April 14, 1865, the very day he was assassinated, **Abraham Lincoln** signed legislation to create the Secret Service. On that fatal night, Lincoln did not want to go to the theater. He had seen *Our American Cousin* once before and was not eager to see it again. But Mary Todd Lincoln had promised his presence, so he attended. As he left, he said, "Good-bye, Crook" to his bodyguard. This puzzled the guard. Ordinarily the president said, "Good night."

- In the weeks following **Abraham Lincoln**'s assassination, many people paid their respects at the White House—and ran off with thousands of dollars of looted objects.

- **Abraham Lincoln**'s eldest son, Robert Todd Lincoln, arrived too late to stop three separate presidential assassinations. He saw his father at Ford's Theater but only after John Wilkes Booth had fired the fatal shot. By invitation, he went to a Washington train station in 1881 to meet **James Garfield**, arriving only minutes after Garfield was shot. Again by invitation, he traveled to Buffalo, New York, in 1901 to meet **William McKinley**, but got there after the fatal shot had already been fired. Robert Todd Lincoln lived for a quarter century after the death of McKinley but made it known that he wanted no further invitations from any president of the United States.

- After **James Garfield** was shot by Charles Guiteau, he spent eighty days on his deathbed while a team of doctors probed him with unwashed hands and unsanitary medical instruments. They tried to find the bullet with a metal detector invented by Alexander Graham Bell, but the device failed because Garfield was placed on a bed with metal springs, and no one thought to move him. To escape the Washington heat, Garfield was moved to a seaside cottage in New Jersey early in September. There he died on September 19, succumbing to death by doctors.

- **William McKinley** became the third president to be assassinated in office. The assassin was an anarchist, Leon Czolgosz, who shot the president in 1901 at the Pan-American Exposition in Buffalo. Virtually the first words out of the president's mouth were to his secretary, George Cortelyou: "My wife—be careful, Cortelyou, how you tell her. Oh, be careful!" When he saw his assassin being beaten to the ground, he cried out, "Don't let them hurt him!"

- Tragically, a back brace that **John F. Kennedy** wore on the day of his assassination actually held him in place as a second and third shot fired by Lee Harvey Oswald riddled his body.

- Ever since the assassination of **John F. Kennedy** on November 22, 1963, historians have pointed out a number of striking similarities between Kennedy's life and death and those of **Abraham Lincoln**. You be the judge as to whether these convergences are significant or mere coincidences:

  ★ Lincoln was elected to the House of Representatives in 1846, Kennedy in 1946. Lincoln failed to win the vice presidential nomination in 1856, Kennedy in 1956. Lincoln was elected to the presidency in 1860, Kennedy in 1960. Lincoln defeated Stephen Douglas, born in 1813; Kennedy defeated **Richard Nixon,** born in 1913. Neither victor received 50 percent of the popular vote. Both presidents lost sons during their

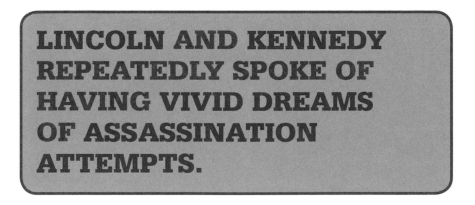

LINCOLN AND KENNEDY REPEATEDLY SPOKE OF HAVING VIVID DREAMS OF ASSASSINATION ATTEMPTS.

presidencies: Willie Lincoln succumbed to typhoid fever, and Patrick Kennedy was stillborn.

* The last names of both presidents are each composed of seven letters. Both presidents had vice presidents named Johnson, both older than their presidents. **Andrew Johnson** was born in 1808, **Lyndon Johnson** in 1908. Andrew Johnson served in the House of Representatives in 1847, Lyndon Johnson in 1947. Both were sitting senators when they became vice president. The first and last names of both vice presidents total an unlucky thirteen letters. Neither Johnson was elected to a second presidential term.

* Lincoln and Kennedy repeatedly spoke of having vivid dreams of assassination attempts. (In a dream, Lincoln heard weeping and wailing over the death of the President. He entered a room and viewed a coffin that contained his own body.) Each was warned by advisers not to attend the fatal event. Both assassins—John Wilkes Booth and Lee Harvey Oswald—were each known by three names totaling fifteen letters.

* Lincoln was assassinated in Ford's Theater, Kennedy in a Ford automobile—a Lincoln. Each was shot in the back of the head, each with his wife nearby. Booth shot Lincoln in a theater and was captured in a barn; Oswald shot Kennedy from a warehouse and was arrested at a theater. Both presidents were assassinated on a Friday. Neither assassin lived to stand trial.

- Six presidents were luckier and survived assassination attempts—**Andrew Jackson, Theodore Roosevelt, Franklin D. Roosevelt, Harry S. Truman, Gerald Ford**, and **Ronald Reagan**.

  ★ **Andrew Jackson** was the target of the first attempted assassination of an American president. On January 30, 1835, a mentally disturbed unemployed house painter named Richard Lawrence fired two different guns at the president from point-blank range. When both weapons failed to fire, Jackson then chased after Lawrence and beat him with his cane. The odds of two consecutive misfires were estimated at 125,000 to 1.

  ★ The only former president to be the target of an attempted assassination, **Theodore Roosevelt** was shot on October 14, 1912, just before giving a speech in Milwaukee during his run as Bull Moose candidate. Even though the bullet lodged four inches deep in his chest, he still delivered the speech. "I don't know whether you fully understand that I have been

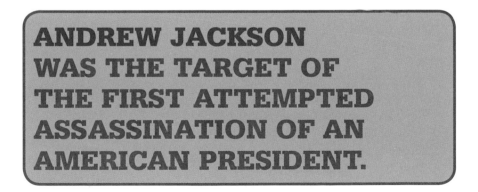

ANDREW JACKSON WAS THE TARGET OF THE FIRST ATTEMPTED ASSASSINATION OF AN AMERICAN PRESIDENT.

GERALD FORD IS THE ONLY PRESIDENT TO HAVE BEEN SHOT AT BY A WOMAN.

shot," he told the stunned audience, "but it takes more than that to kill a Bull Moose." He was saved from certain death by the metal glasses case and the speech text that he had placed in his breast pocket.

★ **Gerald Ford** is the only president to have been shot at by a woman. Lynette "Squeaky" Fromme, a former member of the Charles Manson "family," aimed a pistol at the president but did not get off a shot. Just seventeen days later, Sara Jane Moore fired a bullet at Ford. The bullet struck a nearby taxi driver.

★ When **Ronald Reagan** was shot by would-be assassin John Hinckley Jr. in 1981, he quipped, "I forgot to duck." A few hours after surgery, he quoted Winston Churchill: "There is no more exhilarating feeling than being shot at without result." Two hours later, he laughed, "If I had had this much attention in Hollywood, I'd have stayed there." Reagan is the only sitting president to have been wounded by an assassin's bullet and to have survived.

- To be president is to suffer the slings and arrows of outraged citizens, but several of our presidents have found themselves under fire—and not just by assassins:

  ★ During the Whiskey Rebellion, in 1794, **George Washington** took personal command of the troops to suppress the rebellion. He was fired on by angry rebels.

  ★ During the War of 1812, when the British marched on Washington, **James Madison** was among those who went out to Bladensburg to view the battle. Under fire, he was forced to flee when the American army broke.

  ★ When **Andrew Jackson** was five years old, his mother saw him crying and ordered, "Don't let me see you cry again! Girls were made to cry; boys were made to fight!" Jackson is said to have fought in more than a hundred duels. A bullet from one of those duels remained lodged close to Jackson's heart until the day he died. During the presidential campaign of 1828, the Whigs circulated a thick pamphlet titled *Reminiscences or an Extract from the Catalogue of General Jackson's Youthful Indiscretions, Between the Age of Twenty-Three and Sixty.* The diatribe listed fourteen fights, duels, brawls, and shooting affairs in which Jackson "killed, slashed, and clawed various American citizens."

★ In 1844 Captain Robert Stockton (later of Stockton, California, fame) had a steamship made to his order. He also had a pair of cannon, of 12-inch bore, fabricated, one of his own design and called "The Peacemaker." Stockton took a VIP party out for a cruise on the Potomac River to show off his new ship and entertain his guests by firing his immense gun. The list of dignitaries included the recently widowed president, **John Tyler,** members of Tyler's cabinet, military brass, senators, a former senator, David Gardiner, and his two daughters, Julia and Margaret. After a lunch below, when the guests called for another firing of the gun, President Tyler, deeply in conversation with Julia Gardiner, stayed below. The gun blew up, killing five people in the party and wounding many more, including David Gardiner. President Tyler not only comforted Julia Gardiner, he soon married her. Her conversation with him saved his life.

★ During the Confederate attack on Fort Stevens, **Abraham Lincoln** journeyed to the front to inspect Union defenses. The task of showing him around fell to young Oliver Wendell Holmes Jr., aide to the commanding general, and a future Supreme Court Justice. When Holmes pointed out the enemy in the distance, Lincoln stood up—all 6 feet 3¾ inches of him and a high stovepipe hat, too—to have a look. A snarl of musket fire darted from the enemy trances. Grabbing the president by the arm, Holmes dragged him under cover and shouted, "Get down, you fool!" When he realized what he had said and to whom, Holmes was sure that disciplinary action would follow. But to his immense relief, Lincoln rejoined, "Captain Holmes, I'm glad to see you know how to talk to a civilian."

CHAPTER VI.
PRESIDENTS IN THE MEDIA

IN WARM WEATHER, John Quincy Adams customarily went skinny-dipping in the Potomac River. The first American woman to become a professional journalist, Anne Royall, knew of Adams's 5:00 a.m. swims. After being refused interviews with Adams many times, she went to the river, gathered his clothes, and sat on them until she had her interview from the president, who spoke to her while chin-deep in the water. Before this, no female had interviewed a president.

Until **Abraham Lincoln,** most Americans had no idea what our first fifteen presidents looked and sounded like. Nowadays, with the colossal outreach of mass media, so many of our hopes, dreams, and ideals are inextricably bound up with the persona of the American president.

The presidency can be like a good steak—rare, medium, or well done. Mass media—from portraiture to sculpture, from currency to stamps, from literature to newspapers, from the telephone to radio to television—extend the images and sounds of our chief executives and embedded them in our national consciousness.

- **George Washington** and **James Madison** (whose contributions earned him the title "Father of the Constitution") were the only two presidents to have signed the U.S. Constitution, Madison being the last surviving signer. Washington and Madison are connected in at least one other way: when British troops burned the White House in 1814, **James Madison**'s wife, Dolley, courageously rescued Gilbert Stuart's famous portrait of **George Washington** before she fled the city. That most recognized of all presidential portraits is the only remaining possession from the original building.

- Portraits of presidents **Abraham Lincoln** (on the penny, and the only one facing right), **Thomas Jefferson** (nickel), **Franklin Roosevelt** (dime), **George Washington** (quarter), and **John F. Kennedy** (half-dollar) appear on U.S. coins now in production. In 2007 the government started issuing one-dollar coins featuring images of the American presidents—four each year and in the order of their service.

- Portraits of presidents **George Washington** (on the $1 bill), **Thomas Jefferson** ($2), **Abraham Lincoln** ($5), **Andrew Jackson** ($20), and **Ulysses S. Grant** ($50) appear on U.S. paper currency now in production. Other presidents appeared on denominations no longer produced: **William McKinley** ($500), **Grover Cleveland** ($1,000), **James Madison** ($5,000), and **Woodrow Wilson** ($100,000).

- The images of presidents **George Washington, Thomas Jefferson, Theodore Roosevelt**, and **Abraham Lincoln** (from left to right) appear on Mount Rushmore, located in the Black Hills of South Dakota, twenty-three miles southwest of Rapid City.

- **George Washington**'s profile appears on the Purple Heart.

- Some presidents have known famous authors:

  ★ Nathaniel Hawthorne, author of such American classics as *The Scarlet Letter*, died on a canoe trip in the White Mountains of New Hampshire, accompanied by **Franklin Pierce**. Hawthorne had been Pierce's classmate at Bowdoin College, along with Henry Wadsworth Longfellow.

  ★ **James Garfield** adored the work of General Lew Wallace, the author of *Ben-Hur*. The president appointed Wallace as an ambassador to Constantinople, hoping that the novelist might be inspired to write another exciting book about biblical times. When Charles Dickens toured the United States, Garfield attended his lectures and enjoyed them thoroughly.

  ★ **Theodore Roosevelt** was without doubt one of our most ebullient presidents. The wildly popular British adventure writer Rudyard Kipling spent some time with the president and reported: "I curled up in the seat opposite, and listened and wondered, until the universe seemed to be spinning around, and Theodore was the spinner."

  ★ During the administration of **Dwight Eisenhower**, James Michener, author of *Hawaii, The Source,* and other mega-sellers, was invited to a celebrity dinner at the White House. Michener declined to attend and explained: "Dear Mr. President: I received your invitation three days after I had agreed to speak a few words at a dinner honoring the wonderful high school teacher who taught me how to write. I know you will not miss me at your dinner, but she might at hers." Michener received a handwritten reply from the understanding Ike:

"In his lifetime a man lives under fifteen or sixteen presidents, but a really fine teacher comes into his life but rarely. Go and speak at your teacher's dinner."

- Other presidents have themselves attained literary fame:

  ★ Perhaps the most iconic tale of presidential virtue is that of young **George Washington** admitting to his father that he chopped down a cherry tree in the family garden: "I cannot tell a lie, father, you know I cannot tell a lie! I did cut it with my little hatchet." This episode, which lives on in almost every grammar school across our fair land, is in fact almost certainly fiction. The story was made up out of whole cloth by Parson Mason Locke Weems in his biography *The Life, Death, and Memorable Actions of George Washington*, published immediately after the president's death.

  ★ When the British novelist William Makepeace Thackeray used **George Washington** as a character in *The Virginians*, many Americans were appalled. One critic snapped, "Washington was not like other men, and to bring his character down to the level of the vulgar passions of common life is to give lie to the grandest chapter in the uninspired annals of the human race."

  ★ One of the best known of American poems begins:

    O Captain! my Captain! our fearful trip is done;
    The ship has weathered every rack, the prize we sought is won.

In this poem by Walt Whitman, the captain is **Abraham Lincoln**.

★ As a young man, **Abraham Lincoln** read and re-read the King James Bible, Aesop's Fables, Shakespeare, John Bunyan, Daniel Defoe, and Robert Burns. By the time he became president, he had developed a distinguished prose style of his own—simple, clear, precise, forceful, rhythmic, poetic, and, at times, majestic. **John Adams, Thomas Jefferson, Ulysses S. Grant, Theodore Roosevelt,** and **Woodrow Wilson** all possessed unusual literary skills, but, at his best, Lincoln towered above them all. The critic Jacques Barzun called him a "literary genius."

★ The *Chicago Times* review had this to say about **Abraham Lincoln**'s Gettysburg Address: "The cheek of every American must tingle with shame as he reads the silly, flat and dish-watery utterances of the man who has been pointed out to intelligent foreigners as the President of the United States."

★ The IRS Form 1040 EZ contains 418 words and the back of a Lay's Potato Chips bag has 401. In the brief compass of 272 words, President Lincoln transformed a gruesome battle into the raison d'être of a truly *United* States that for the first time in its history became a union. Before Lincoln, people used "the United States" as a plural: "The United States *are...*" Ever after it would be "The United States *is...*" That same day at Gettysburg, November 19, 1864, Edward Everett, famed for his oratory, spoke for close to two hours, while Lincoln took only a couple of minutes. Afterwards, Everett took Lincoln aside and said, "My speech will soon be forgotten; yours never will. How gladly would I exchange my hundred pages for your twenty lines!"

★ Even while a sundered nation was slaughtering itself on the battlefields of the Civil War, Lincoln could still find time, on November 21, 1864, to write this letter to Lydia Bixby: "Dear Madam: I have been shown in the files of the War Department a statement of the Adjutant-General of Massachusetts that you are the mother of five sons who have died gloriously on the field of battle. I feel how weak and fruitless must be any words of mine which should attempt to beguile you from the grief of a loss so overwhelming. But I cannot refrain from tendering to you the consolation that may be found in the thanks of the Republic they died to save. I pray that our Heavenly Father may assuage the anguish of your bereavement, and leave you only the cherished memory of the loved and lost, and the solemn pride that must be yours to have laid so costly a sacrifice upon the altar of freedom. Yours very sincerely and respectfully, A. Lincoln"

★ **Ulysses S. Grant** finished his 200,000-word *Memoirs* only a few days before his death, so he never saw the work published. The book ultimately brought in $500,000 for his family. It remains one of the finest accounts of the Civil War ever written. Grant's popular autobiography was published by his friend Mark Twain in 1885, the same year that Twain came out with *The Adventures of Huckleberry Finn*.

★ **Herbert Hoover** wrote approximately sixteen books, including one called *Fishing for Fun and to Wash Your Soul*.

★ **John F. Kennedy** is the only president to receive the Pulitzer Prize—for his book *Profiles in Courage*.

* **Jimmy Carter** is our most writerly president, having published about twenty books, many of which have been best sellers. Carter wrote most of his books after his presidency and some with his wife, Rosalynn, as co-author. In 2003, Carter published a novel, *The Hornet's Nest*, a fictional story of the Revolutionary War in the South. Carter remains the only president to have published a novel.

- The first telephone was installed in the White House in 1879. **Rutherford B. Hayes** was the first president to use a telephone while in office. **Grover Cleveland** personally answered the White House phone. **Calvin Coolidge** hated telephones and never answered them. **William McKinley** was the first president to campaign by telephone.

- **Abraham Lincoln** is the president most portrayed in the movies, but at least two of our presidents have acted in dramatic films:

    * **Grover Cleveland** was our first presidential movie star. In 1895, Cleveland agreed to be filmed signing a bill into law. The movie was called *A Capital Courtship*, and it was a big hit on the Lyceum circuit.

    * **Ronald Reagan** was our only president to have been a professional actor, appearing in fifty-four Hollywood films. Reagan and his second wife, Nancy Davis, appeared opposite each other in the movie *Hellcats of the Navy*. Asked if he had been nervous debating Jimmy Carter, Reagan smiled, "No, not at all. I've been on the same stage with John Wayne." In one of his films, *The Winning Team*, Reagan played Philadelphia Nationals

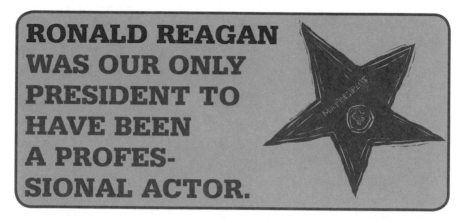

RONALD REAGAN WAS OUR ONLY PRESIDENT TO HAVE BEEN A PROFESSIONAL ACTOR.

pitcher Grover Cleveland Alexander. Thus, a president played the role of a character with a president's name.

★ Conversely, an actor who was not a president (but whose name consists of those of three presidents) played the movie role of a president. Megastar Harrison Ford (there were two presidents Harrison and one president Ford) played President James Marshall in the movie *Air Force One*. **Ronald Reagan** and Harrison Ford are joined in another way: Harrison Ford starred in the early *Star Wars* films, and Reagan was a staunch proponent of the Star Wars anti-missile defense system.

• **Theodore Roosevelt** was the first president to use the privately owned press to communicate frequently with the public. As such, he was the founder of the presidential press conference. One rainy day he looked out the window and saw a group of reporters manning their usual post by the White

House gates. Their purpose was to question those entering and leaving the White House in order to gain leads for news stories. Seeing them wet, cold, and miserable, Roosevelt invited them in and ordered that a room be set aside for them. In doing so, he granted the press a status it had never before enjoyed and that it has never since relinquished:

★ While TR's press conferences were usually one-way lectures, often while the president was under the blade of his barber's razor, **Woodrow Wilson** instituted the practice of holding regular press conferences open to all accredited reporters, not just ones hand-picked by the president and his staff. Unlike TR, he did not direct discussion and allowed reporters to ask their questions. These innovations reduced the power of the president over the news generated by presidential press conference.

★ **Warren G. Harding**, a former newspaperman himself, made the press conference an official duty of his administration.

★ During his 1924 presidential campaign, reporters eagerly sought out **Calvin Coolidge.** "Have you any statement about the campaign? " asked one reporter. "No," answered Coolidge. "Can you tell us something about the world situation?" "No." "Any information about the world situation?" "No." As the disappointed reporters started to leave, Coolidge said solemnly, "Now, remember—don't quote me."

★ **Franklin D. Roosevelt** conducted press conferences twice a week, every week—nine hundred and ninety-two sessions—through wartime and personal illness.

★ Reporters were so put off at **Dwight Eisenhower**'s habit of rambling at press conferences that one of them rewrote the Gettysburg Address in the meandering style that Ike might have delivered it. The parody begins: "I haven't checked these figures, but eighty-seven years ago, I think it was, a number of individuals organized a government setup here in this country. I believe it covered certain eastern areas, with the idea they were following up, based on a sort of national independence arrangement. . . ."

★ At his farewell to the press corps, **Richard Nixon** lashed out, "But as I leave you, I want you to know—just think how much you're going to be missing. You won't have Nixon to kick around anymore because, gentlemen, this is my last press conference."

★ **John F. Kennedy** was the first president to conduct press conferences on live television.

★ **Ronald Reagan** turned seventy in February 1981 and joked about his age in a speech to the Washington Press Club. "I know your organization was founded in 1919," he remarked. Then, after a slight pause, he added, "It seems like only yesterday."

• As the twentieth century gathered momentum, radio became a significant medium through which to communicate the mind and heart of the presidency:

★ **Warren G. Harding** was the first president to own a radio and the first to speak over the radio airwaves, with the aid of a long-distance wireless telephone.

★ **Franklin D. Roosevelt**'s fireside chats were a series of thirty evening radio talks given between 1933 and 1944. Originally designed to garner support for his New Deal policies during the Great Depression, these evening radio talks to the American public were broadcast straight from the White House. The addresses gave people a sense of hope and security during difficult times and helped keep Roosevelt popular despite the continuing Depression. Because nearly every home in working-class neighborhoods had the radio on and windows open in summertime, it was possible to take a long walk without missing many of the president's words.

FRANKLIN D. ROOSEVELT'S FIRESIDE CHATS WERE A SERIES OF THIRTY EVENING RADIO TALKS.

• The assassination and funeral of **John F. Kennedy** marked a turning point in American history. It was the first time that virtually the entire nation came together to witness a national tragedy, and the witnessing was through television. The live coverage and images of those events—the shooting of Lee Harvey

THE ASSASSINATION AND FUNERAL OF JOHN F. KENNEDY MARKED A TURNING POINT IN AMERICAN HISTORY.

Oswald, the funeral cortege, the black-veiled widow, and the president's tiny son, John John, saluting the flag—seared the national psyche and established television as an archetypal source of news. Television has become, perhaps, the most powerful and pervasive medium during the past fifty years:

★ **Herbert Hoover** appeared on the nation's first television broadcast in 1927, but as Secretary of Commerce, not as president.

★ The first president to appear on television during his presidency was **Franklin D. Roosevelt**. He was seen by American viewers at the opening of the New York World's Fair on April 30, 1939.

★ **Dwight Eisenhower** was the first president to appear on color television.

★ The Kennedy-Nixon debates in 1960, watched by seventy million viewers, marked the grand entrance of television into the presidential politics.

Most experts credit **John F. Kennedy**'s successful TV-friendly performances in the four debates as a significant factor in his subsequent election. Tellingly, most polls indicated that **Richard Nixon** won the radio versions of those exchanges.

★ During 1975–76, the first year of the cutting and cutting-edge television show *Saturday Night Live*, comedian Chevy Chase spoofed **Gerald Ford** by falling down a lot, and spectacularly. Chase's widely watched schtick was a take-off on news footage that showed Ford stumbling on several occasions. **Jimmy Carter**'s razor-thin victory in 1976 over Ford, one of our nation's most athletic and fittest presidents, may have been significantly influenced by Chase's depicting him as a stumblebum.

★ Many would support **Ronald Reagan** as our most television-savy president. In his 1980 debates with **Jimmy Carter,** Reagan, at the end of the exchange, made sure to walk across the dais to shake hands with Carter to show that Reagan was clearly taller, and hence the more commanding of the two.

★ In his televised presidential debate against his considerably younger opponent, Walter Mondale, **Ronald Reagan** quipped, "I will not make age an issue in this campaign. I am not going to exploit, for political purposes, my opponent's youth and inexperience."

pre sident

CHAPTER VII.
MORE FASCINATING
FACTS ABOUT
OUR PRESIDENTS

THE CURTISS CANDY COMPANY claimed that its Baby Ruth candy bar, put on the market in 1921, was named after Ruth Cleveland, daughter of **Grover Cleveland.** In fact, although never proved in a court of law, the confection played off the name of baseball slugger Babe Ruth. Naming a candy bar after the long-dead daughter of a long-ago president—a daughter who died at the age of twelve from diphtheria in 1904—would have been a bizarre choice.

That a candy bar named "Baby Ruth" appeared on the market just when a baseball player named Babe Ruth was becoming the most famous person in America raises our collective eyebrow even higher. Ironically, when a candy-making competitor secured Babe Ruth's permission to manufacture a confection named the "Babe Ruth Home Run Bar," Curtiss successfully sued to have the bar barred because the name too closely resembled that of their own product! So the Babe never collected a penny for either clump of candy.

Years later, the same Babe Ruth was asked by a reporter how the star slugger could demand an $80,000 annual salary when **Herbert Hoover** was making only $75,000. Ruth replied, "I know, but I had a better year than Hoover."

Those are the kinds of colorful and quirky facts about presidents that fail to make it into the pages of our textbooks. Here are some bits of presidential trivia that you may not have learned in your high school or college American history courses:

- While Congress wished to address him as "His Highness, the President of the United States of America and the Protector of Their Liberties," **George Washington** opted for, and established the tradition of, "Mr. President."

- As the American minister to France, Benjamin Franklin attended a diplomatic dinner shortly after the American Revolutionary War ended. The French foreign minister opened the dinner by offering a champagne toast to his King: "To His Majesty, Louis the Sixteenth, who, like the moon, fills the earth with a soft, benevolent glow." The British ambassador then rose to give his toast: "To George the Third, who like the sun at noonday, spreads his light and illumines the world." Then the aging Franklin exulted: "I cannot give you the sun or the moon, but I give you **George Washington,** General of the Armies of the United States, who, like Joshua of old, commanded both the sun and the moon to stand still, and both obeyed!"

- **John Adams** was the great-great-grandson of John and Priscilla Alden, pilgrims who landed at Plymouth Rock in 1620.

- When **Thomas Jefferson** took office in 1801, there were almost 900,000 slaves in a population of about 5,500,000 Americans. Jefferson owned approximately two hundred slaves. Jefferson died $107,000 in debt, a defect partially alleviated by the sale of his slaves.

- **Thomas Jefferson** was the principal founder of the Library of Congress. **Millard Fillmore** and his cabinet helped fight the Library of Congress fire of 1851, which destroyed the majority of the collection, many donated by or bought from Jefferson.

- **Thomas Jefferson** was the first American to introduce french fried potatoes, at a dinner party.

- **James Monroe**'s daughter, Maria, was the first bride to be married in the White House.

- **John Quincy Adams** argued before the Supreme Court on behalf of slaves from the ship *Amistad,* who mutinied during their journey from Africa.

- A telegram informing **Zachary Taylor** that he had been nominated for the presidency by the Whig party was returned by the mail service. Taylor learned of the nomination in the newspaper.

- **Millard Fillmore** refused an honorary degree from Oxford University because he felt he had "neither literary nor scientific attainment." He added that no one should accept a degree that he couldn't actually read.

- **Franklin Pierce** won the presidency by defeating his old commanding officer from the Mexican War, Winfield Scott.

- **Andrew Johnson** is buried beneath a willow tree that he planted. As he requested, his head rests on a copy of the Constitution.

- **Ulysses S. Grant**, so powerfully associated with the mass slaughters of the Civil War, was nauseated at the sight of blood, disliked hunting, abhorred cruelty to animals, and was sickened by the spectacle of a bullfight in Mexico.

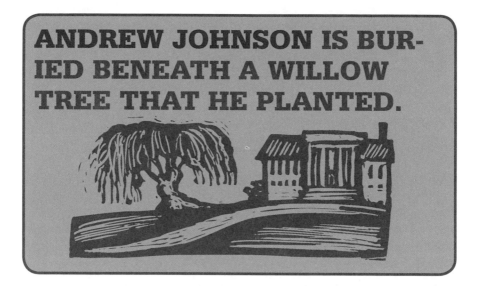

**ANDREW JOHNSON IS BUR-
IED BENEATH A WILLOW
TREE THAT HE PLANTED.**

- During his term of office, **Ulysses S. Grant** was once arrested and fined $20 for exceeding the Washington speed limit on his horse. When the embarrassed policeman realized that he was dealing with the president, he hesitated to issue the ticket. But President Grant insisted on paying the fine and wrote a letter to the Washington Police Department complimenting the officer on his fine sense of duty.

- "Who is buried in Grant's Tomb?" You may think that you know the answer to that old question, which Groucho Marx popularized on his quiz show, *You Bet Your Life,* to ensure that each contestant won at least fifty dollars. But even visitors who are standing inside the magnificent monument often answer the riddle incorrectly. In a remote corner of bustling New York City, on a quiet bluff along the Hudson River far from Times Square and Broadway, **Ulysses S. Grant** and his wife, Julia Dent, lie in a stately marble mausoleum. The monument was dedicated on the president's seventy-fifth birthday, April 27, 1897, almost twelve years after he had died. Five years later, his wife passed and was put to rest next to him. So you might think the answer to Groucho's question, "Who is buried in Grant's tomb?" would be "President and Mrs. Grant." Wrong again. The actual answer to the famous poser is that nobody is buried in Grant's Tomb. The Grants are entombed therein, not buried.

- **Grover Cleveland** dedicated the Statue of Liberty on October 28, 1886.

- **Theodore Roosevelt** was concerned that many young men were being severely injured, and in some cases killed, as a result of the rough and violent new contact sport called football. He petitioned to have the game banned in the United States, but the sport was too popular. As a result of his efforts, however, new rules were adopted and safety gear such as helmets was encouraged.

- **Calvin Coolidge**, a man of few words, was so famous for saying so little that a White House dinner guest made a bet that she could get the president to say more than two words. She told the president of her wager. His reply: "You lose."

- According to *Presidential Doodles* (Basic Books, 2006), **Herbert Hoover** was the most artistic and productive doodler among our chief executives.

- Anticipating a victory for **Harry S. Truman**'s opponent, Thomas E. Dewey, the *Chicago Daily Tribune* printed the headline DEWEY DEFEATS TRUMAN on the front page of its 1948 postelection edition—but Truman won. Stunned by his defeat, Dewey sighed that he felt like the man who woke up to find himself inside a coffin with a lily in his hand and thought, "If I'm alive, what am I doing here? And if I'm dead, why do I have to go to the bathroom?"

- **Harry S. Truman** would regularly arise at 5:00 a.m. to practice the piano for two hours.

- A graduate of West Point, **Dwight Eisenhower** was the last U.S. general (and the only one in the twentieth century) to become president. In World War II he was in charge of the D-Day invasion in 1944 and served as commander in chief of the allies in Europe. His parents were members of a fundamentalist religious sect and were strict pacifists.

- **Dwight Eisenhower** played football at West Point and was injured trying to tackle Olympic and NFL star Jim Thorpe.

- In 1962, **John F. Kennedy** entertained a group of Nobel Prize winners at the White House. He heralded the event as the most distinguished gathering of intellectual talent ever brought together in the Executive Mansion— except for when **Thomas Jefferson** dined alone. In addition to Jefferson's political contributions, described throughout this book, our third president designed many of the first buildings of the University of Virginia, which he founded, and two of his other architectural designs—Monticello and Bremo—are still among the most exquisite country houses in America. He had much to do with the planning of Washington, D.C., and invented a collapsible writing table and a pedometer to measure his walks.

- **Lyndon Johnson** was the youngest Senate majority leader.

- **Lyndon Johnson** and his wife, Lady Bird, held a Festival of the Arts at the White House, the first of its kind. At the festival, Sarah Vaughan, the great jazz singer, held her distinguished audience rapt for a half hour. As the party was breaking up, a White House staffer found Miss Vaughan weeping in her dressing room. "What's the matter?" asked the staffer. "Nothing is the matter," said the singer. "It's just that twenty years ago, when I came to Washington, I couldn't even get a hotel room. But tonight, I sang for the President of the United States—and then he asked me to dance with him. It is more than I can stand."

- **Richard Nixon** received a gold-plated 45-caliber pistol as a gift from Elvis Presley.

- When he received his commission in 1943, **George H. W. Bush** became, at nineteen, the youngest pilot then in the U.S. Navy. He flew fifty-eight combat missions during World War II. He romantically painted the name "Barbara" on the side of his bomber.

CHAPTER VIII.
INAUGURATIONS:
OMENS OF THINGS TO COME

THE STORY BEHIND the word *inaugurate* is an intriguing one. It literally means "to take omens from the flight of birds." In ancient Rome, augurs would predict the outcome of an enterprise by the way the birds were flying. After studying the formations of the birds on the wing, these soothsayer-magicians would tell a general whether or not to march or to do battle. They might even catch one of these birds and cut it open to observe its entrails for omens.

Nowadays, presidential candidates use their inauguration speeches to take flight on an updraft of words rather than birds—and they do often spill their guts for all to see. It all began with **George Washington**, whose first inaugural began this way: "Among the vicissitudes incident to life no event could have filled me with greater anxieties than that of which the notification was transmitted by your order, and received on the fourteenth day of the present month. On the one hand, I was summoned by my country, whose voice I can never hear but with veneration and love, from a retreat which I had chosen with the fondest predilection, and, in my flattering hopes, with an immutable decision, as the asylum of my declining years."

The shortest inauguration speech of all American presidents, only 133 words, was delivered by **George Washington** at his second inaugural on March 4, 1793. **Abraham Lincoln**'s second inaugural address was the second shortest.

The longest inauguration address, delivered by **William Henry Harrison** on March 4, 1841, contained 8,443 words.

Washington's speech lasted about two minutes; Harrison's speech took about an hour and forty minutes to deliver.

The fact that the longest speech preceded the shortest presidential term in American history was no coincidence. Harrison delivered his message outdoors on the east portico of the Capitol. In spite of the cold and stormy day, Harrison refused to wear a hat or coat. (Having studied medicine for a year at the University of Pennsylvania, Harrison should have known better.) He caught a cold that developed into pneumonia, from which he died in the White House on April 4, 1841, a scant thirty-one days after he had been sworn in.

Moral: Wear your galoshes and keep your speeches short.

Here are some inaugural firsts:

- **George Washington** set the precedents of kissing the Bible after the oath and of presenting an inaugural speech. His was written primarily by **James Madison.**

- **John Adams** was the first president to receive the oath from the chief justice of the United States (Oliver Ellsworth). No chief justice has ever missed a presidential swearing-in ceremony.

- **Thomas Jefferson** was the first president to be inaugurated at the Capitol in Washington, D.C.

- The first inaugural ball was held for **James Madison.**

- The War of 1812 and World War II forced the swearings-in of **James Madison** and **Franklin D. Roosevelt** to be held at other locations than Washington, D.C.

- The inauguration of **James Monroe** was the first to be held outdoors.

- **Martin Van Buren**'s inauguration marked the first time that outgoing and incoming presidents (**Andrew Jackson** and Van Buren) rode together in a carriage to the Capitol for the event. Two other memorable rides through the Washington streets occurred:

  ★ In 1921, outgoing President **Woodrow Wilson** and incoming President **Warren G. Harding** took the inaugural ride together. Both men raised their hats and waved to the cheering crowds. On this greatest day of his life, people-person Harding wanted to wave to every soul on earth. But he noticed that the waving caused considerable pain to the stroke-afflicted Wilson. Harding stopped waving so that the debilitated Wilson could also stop.

  ★ Probably the most uncomfortable pairing of outgoing and incoming presidents was in 1933, when **Herbert Hoover,** depressed by the Depression, and **Franklin D. Roosevelt** rode together to Roosevelt's inauguration. Gloomy and silent, Hoover knew that the adoring crowds were cheering optimistically for his dashing successor.

- **James Polk**'s inauguration was the first to be reported by telegraph.

JAMES BUCHANAN'S INAUGURATION WAS THE FIRST TO BE PHOTOGRAPHED.

- **Franklin Pierce** was the first president to memorize his inaugural address—a 3,319-word speech that he delivered without the aid of notes.

- **Abraham Lincoln**'s second inauguration marked the first time that African Americans participated in the inaugural parade.

- **Ulysses S. Grant** was the first president whose father and mother were alive at the time of his inauguration. **John F. Kennedy** and **George W. Bush** were also fortunate enough to have both parents live long enough to see them become president, and their parents actually attended the ceremonies.

- **James Garfield**'s mother was the first to attend her son's inauguration.

- **William McKinley**'s inauguration was the first to be recorded by movie camera.

- **William Howard Taft**'s inauguration was the first time that a president's wife rode with her husband in the procession from the Capitol to the White House.

- The inaugurations of **William Howard Taft** in 1909 and **Ronald Reagan** in 1985 had to be moved indoors at the Capitol, because of frigid weather.

- **Woodrow Wilson**'s inauguration was the first time that women participated in the inaugural parade.

- **Warren G. Harding** was the first president to ride to and from his inauguration in an automobile.

- **John F. Kennedy**'s inauguration marked the first time a poet, Robert Frost, participated in the official ceremonies at the Capitol. **Bill Clinton** was the only other president to feature poets at his inauguration—Maya Angelou at his first and Miller Williams at his second.

HARRY S. TRUMAN'S INAUGURATION WAS THE FIRST TO BE TELEVISED.

- After hearing **John F. Kennedy**'s inaugural address, **Richard Nixon** remarked to Ted Sorensen, a Kennedy aide, "I wish I had said some of those things." "What part?" Sorensen wanted to know. "The part about 'ask not what your country can do for you . . .'?"
  "No," said Nixon. "The part that starts, 'I do solemnly swear'."

- **Jimmy Carter** was the first president sworn in by his nickname. His Inauguration Day parade featured a giant peanut-shaped balloon.

- The inauguration of **Ronald Reagan** was the biggest, fanciest, and costliest in American history. Comedian Johnny Carson observed wryly, "This is the first administration to have a premiere."

- Forty million jelly beans were consumed at **Ronald Reagan**'s inaugural, almost the number of votes he received in the election.

- **Bill Clinton**'s inaugural was the first to be broadcast live on the Internet and the first to fall on the Martin Luther King Jr. holiday.

Quick: Name a president who did not deliver an inaugural address.

Actually, you have a choice of five. Presidents **John Tyler, Millard Fillmore, Andrew Johnson, Chester A. Arthur,** and **Gerald Ford** did not deliver inaugural speeches because they were never elected to the presidency.

Here are some more inaugural onlys and oddities:

- Except for **George Washington**'s first inaugural, when he was sworn in on April 30, 1789, all presidents until 1937 were inaugurated in March in an effort to avoid bad weather. Washington's inauguration was more than a month late because the United States Congress had not properly convened, so his first term was that much shorter than his second. The Twentieth Amendment changed the inaugural date to January 20. **Franklin D. Roosevelt**'s second inauguration was the first to be held on that date.

- Both Adamses, father and son, made it a point to leave Washington the day before their successors' inaugurations.

- **Thomas Jefferson** was the only president to walk to and from his inauguration.

- Colorful **Andrew Jackson** invited any and all of his fellow Tennesseeans to his inauguration party at the White House. "It was like the inundation of the northern barbarians into Rome," wrote one eyewitness, "save that the tumultuous tide came in from a different point of the compass. The West and the South seemed to have precipitated themselves upon the North and overwhelmed it." Ruffians knocked the trays out of waiters' hand, smashed china and glassware, overturned furniture, brushed bric-a-brac from mantels, spilled whiskey and chicken and spat tobacco juice on the carpets, and stood with muddy boots on damask-covered chairs to get a good look at "Old Hickory." The festivities got so out of hand, including extensive monetary damage to the furnishings, that the president left the party and spent the night at a Washington hotel.

- In at least one way, **Zachary Taylor** became the darling of trivia buffs. In March 1849 he refused to be inaugurated and take the oath of office on a Sunday because of his religious beliefs. The offices of President and Vice President were vacant at the time, so someone had to be the president, but who? David Rice Atchison, the President Pro Tempore of the Senate, was sworn in as president. He didn't do much. When asked what he did that day, he said, "I went to bed. There had been two or three busy nights finishing up the work of the Senate, and I slept most of that Sunday."

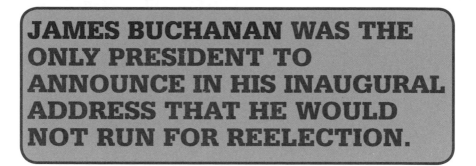

JAMES BUCHANAN WAS THE ONLY PRESIDENT TO ANNOUNCE IN HIS INAUGURAL ADDRESS THAT HE WOULD NOT RUN FOR REELECTION.

- **Rutherford B. Hayes** was the only president to take the oath of office in the White House. Afraid of violent disruption at a public inauguration after the most contentious election in American history, President **Ulysses S. Grant** invited Hayes to the White House, where he was administered the oath of office in the Red Room. Democrats boycotted the inauguration.

- **Chester A. Arthur** took the oath of office in his own home.

- In 1923, upon the death of President Harding, **Calvin Coolidge** was sworn in by his father, a notary public. The elder Coolidge read the oath of office to his son by the light of a kerosene lamp in the parlor of a remote Vermont farmhouse. In 1925 Coolidge was administered the oath of office by an ex-president, **William Howard Taft,** who was then chief justice of the Supreme Court. Coolidge's inauguration was also the first to be broadcast nationally by radio. **Herbert Hoover** was also sworn in by Chief Justice Taft, in 1929.

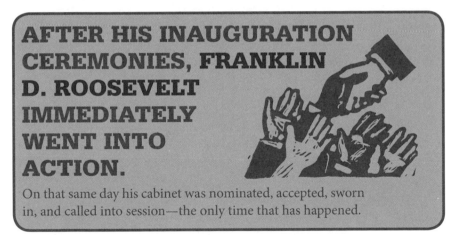

AFTER HIS INAUGURATION CEREMONIES, FRANKLIN D. ROOSEVELT IMMEDIATELY WENT INTO ACTION.

On that same day his cabinet was nominated, accepted, sworn in, and called into session—the only time that has happened.

- **Lyndon Johnson**'s inauguration was the only time that the oath was administered in an airplane (Air Force One, a Boeing 707, at Love Field in Dallas,

Texas) and the only time that the oath was administered by a woman, Sarah T. Hughes, U. S. district judge of the Northern District of Texas. Johnson and **Ronald Reagan** were the only presidents to be sworn in with their wives holding the Bible.

- The warmest January inauguration on record was **Ronald Reagan**'s first: 55 degrees, the coldest his second: 7 degrees.

Here are statements culled from the inaugural addresses of some twentieth-century American presidents. Identify each president.

QUIZ

1. "We are provincials no longer. The tragic events of the thirty months of vital turmoil through which we have just passed have made us citizens of the world. There can be no turning back. Our own fortunes as a nation are involved whether we would have it so or not."

2. "There would be little traffic in illegal liquor if only criminals patronized it. We must awake to the fact that this patronage from large numbers of law-abiding citizens is supplying the rewards and stimulating crime."

3. "First of all, let me assert my firm belief that the only thing we have to fear is fear itself—nameless, unreasoning, unjustified terror which paralyzes needed efforts to convert retreat into advance."

4. "And so, my fellow Americans: Ask not what your country can do for you—ask what you can do for your country."

5. "Now, so there will be no misunderstanding, it's not my intention to do away with government. It is rather to make it work with us, not over us; to stand by our side, not ride on our back. Government can and must provide opportunity, not smother it; foster productivity, not stifle it."

Answers
1. Woodrow Wilson | 2. Herbert Hoover | 3. Franklin D. Roosevelt | 4. John F. Kennedy | 5. Ronald Reagan

CHAPTER IX.
PRESIDENTIAL NICKNAMES

THEODORE ROOSEVELT (he roundly disliked the nickname "Teddy") was our initial president to be identified at times by his initials, *TR*. FDR, JFK, and LBJ followed TR's lead.

But a more famous set of initials were attached to an earlier president.

In the 1830s, in New England, there was a craze for initialisms, in the manner of *FYI*, *PDQ*, *aka*, and *TGIF*, so popular today. The fad went so far as to generate letter combinations of intentionally comic misspellings: *KG* for "know go," *KY* for "know yuse," *NSMJ* for "'nough said 'mong jentlemen," and *OR* for "oll rong." *OK* for "oll korrect" naturally followed.

Of all those loopy initialisms and facetious misspellings *OK* alone survived. That's because of a presidential nickname that consolidated the letters in the national memory. **Martin Van Buren,** elected our eighth president in 1836, was born in Kinderhook, New York, and, early in his political career, he was dubbed "Old Kinderhook." Echoing the "Oll Korrect" initialism, *OK* became the rallying cry of the Old Kinderhook Club, a Democratic organization supporting Van Buren during the 1840 campaign. Thus, the accident of Van Buren's birthplace rescued *OK* from the dustbin of history.

OK BECAME THE RALLYING CRY OF THE OLD KINDER-HOOK CLUB, A DEMOCRATIC ORGANIZATION SUPPORTING VAN BUREN DURING THE 1840 CAMPAIGN.

The coinage did Van Buren no good, and he was defeated in his bid for reelection. But the word honoring his name today remains what H. L. Mencken identified as "the most shining and successful Americanism ever invented."

Match the presidential nicknames in the left-hand column with the presidents in the second column:

1. The Great Emancipator   a. James Buchanan
2. Old Hickory   b. Calvin Coolidge
3. The Father of His Country   c. Dwight D. Eisenhower
4. The Sage of Monticello   d. Ulysses S. Grant
5. Ike   e. William Henry Harrison
6. The King of Camelot   f. Andrew Jackson
7. Tricky Dicky   g. Thomas Jefferson
8. Silent Cal   h. John F. Kennedy
9. Tippecanoe   i. Abraham Lincoln
10. Unconditional Surrender   j. Richard M. Nixon
11. Old Rough and Ready   k. Ronald Reagan
12. The Gipper   l. Franklin D. Roosevelt
13. The New Dealer   m. Theodore Roosevelt
14. The Schoolmaster   n. William Howard Taft
15. The Rough Rider   o. Zachary Taylor
16. Big Bill   p. Harry S Truman
17. The Bachelor President   q. George Washington
18. The Haberdasher   r. Woodrow Wilson

Answers
1. i | 2. f | 3. q | 4. g | 5. c | 6. h | 7. j | 8. b | 9. e |
10. d | 11. o | 12. k | 13. l | 14. r | 15. m | 16. n |
17. a | 18. p

CHAPTER X.
RIGHT DOWN
THE MIDDLE

PRESIDENTS HAVE MORE than their share of intriguing middle names.

Two of them—**Ronald** *Wilson* **Reagan** and **William** *Jefferson* **Clinton**—match the last names of two of their predecessors.

Ulysses S. Grant came into this world as Hiram Ulysses Grant. When his name was mistakenly entered on the West Point register as *Ulysses S. Grant*, he eagerly embraced the error because he detested the initials H. U. G. and loved having the initials U.S., as in "Unconditional Surrender," "United States," and "Uncle Sam."

Less pyrotechnically, Grover was originally the middle name of Stephen **Grover Cleveland,** Woodrow the middle name of Thomas **Woodrow Wilson,** Calvin the middle name of John **Calvin Coolidge,** and Dwight the middle name of David **Dwight Eisenhower.**

And then there's **Harry S. Truman**—or is it Harry S Truman, without the period? Truman initiated this punctuation controversy in 1962, when he told reporters that the *S* wasn't an initial for a particular name. Rather, the *S* was a compromise between the names of his grandfathers, Anderson Shipp Truman and Solomon Young, making the letter a kind of embracive middle name.

But Truman himself usually placed a period after the *S*, and the most authoritative style manuals recommend its use in the interest of consistency, even if the initial does not appear to stand for any particular name.

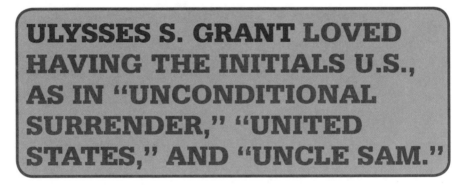

ULYSSES S. GRANT LOVED HAVING THE INITIALS U.S., AS IN "UNCONDITIONAL SURRENDER," "UNITED STATES," AND "UNCLE SAM."

QUIZ

Using each middle name listed, identify the full name of each American president:

1. Abram
2. Alan
3. Baines
4. Birchard
5. Clark
6. Delano
7. Earl
8. Fitzgerald

9. Gamaliel
10. Henry
11. Herbert Walker
12. Howard
13. Knox
14. Milhous
15. Quincy
16. Walker

Answers

1. James Abram Garfield | 2. Chester Alan Arthur | 3. Lyndon Baines Johnson | 4. Rutherford Birchard Hayes | 5. Herbert Clark Hoover | 6. Franklin Delano Roosevelt | 7. James Earl Carter | 8. John Fitzgerald Kennedy | 9. Warren Gamaliel Harding | 10. William Henry Harrison | 11. George Herbert Walker Bush (our only president to be identified with two middle names) | 12. William Howard Taft | 13. James Knox Polk | 14. Richard Milhous Nixon | 15. John Quincy Adams | 16. George Walker Bush.

hello, my name is

Mr. President

CHAPTER XI.
WHAT'S IN A
PRESIDENT'S NAME?

AN ANAGRAM is the rearrangement of all the letters in a word or phrase to create another word or phrase. Here are the best efforts to anagram the names of our twentieth- and twenty-first-century presidents. Some work better grammatically than others; some are more appropriate to the president, some less telling.

Theodore Roosevelt • LOVED HORSE; TREE, TOO

William Howard Taft • A WORD WITH ALL: I'M FAT

Woodrow Wilson • O LORD , SO NOW WWI

Warren Gamaliel Harding • REAL WINNER? HIM A LAGGARD

Calvin Coolidge • LOVE? A COLD ICING

Herbert Clark Hoover • O, HARK, CLEVER BROTHER

Franklin Delano Roosevelt • ELEANOR, KIN, LAST FOND LOVER

Harry S. Truman • RASH ARMY RUNT

Dwight David Eisenhower • HE DID VIEW THE WAR DOINGS

John Fitzgerald Kennedy • ZING! JOY DARKEN, THEN FLED

Lyndon Baines Johnson • NO NINNY, HE'S ON JOB LADS

Richard Milhous Nixon • HUSH—NIX CRIMINAL ODOR

Gerald Rudolph Ford • A RUDER LORD; GOLF PH.D.

James Earl Carter • A RARE, CALM JESTER

Ronald W. Reagan • A WAN OLD RANGER

George Bush • HE BUGS GORE

William Jefferson Clinton • JILTS NICE WOMEN; IN FOR FALL

George W. Bush • HE GREW BOGUS

In honor of our first president, here's a stately sonnet composed by David Shulman way back in 1936. Each line is an anagram (a rearrangement) of all the letters in the title, yet the lines are cast in reasonable meter and each couplet rhymes!

Washington Crossing the Delaware

A hard, howling, tossing, water scene;
Strong tide was washing hero clean.
How cold! Weather stings as in anger.
O silent night shows war ace danger!

The cold waters swashing on in rage.
Redcoats warn slow his hint engage.
When general's star wish'd "Go!"
He saw his ragged continentals row.

Ah, he stands—sailor crew went going,
And so this general watches rowing.
He hastens—Winter again grows cold;
A wet crew gain Hessian stronghold.

George can't lose war with 's hands in;
He's astern—so, go alight, crew, and win!

What is the most popular first name among presidents? The answer is *James.* Six presidents share that first name—Madison, Monroe, Polk, Buchanan, Garfield, and Carter. Tied for second place are *William* with four—Harrison, McKinley, Taft, and Clinton—and *John* with four—Adams, Quincy Adams, Tyler, and Kennedy. Massachusetts is the birth state of three presidents named John—**John Adams, John Quincy Adams,** and **John F. Kennedy.** In 2004, Senator John Kerry failed in his bid to become the fourth.

Despite fourteen presidents with the first names James, John, and William, twenty of our chief executives, starting with **Thomas Jefferson** and ending with **Ronald Reagan,** have first names not shared by any other man in the office.

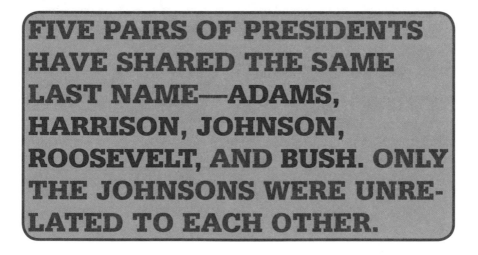

FIVE PAIRS OF PRESIDENTS HAVE SHARED THE SAME LAST NAME—ADAMS, HARRISON, JOHNSON, ROOSEVELT, AND BUSH. ONLY THE JOHNSONS WERE UNRELATED TO EACH OTHER.

Here are some other letter-perfect tidbits of presidential trivia:

- Five presidential last names consist of four letters. In chronological order, they are *Polk, Taft, Ford, Bush,* and *Bush.* **George W. Bush** is the only one among them to serve two terms.

- In contrast to the monosyllabic monikers above, *Eisenhower* is the only presidential surname that contains four syllables and that begins with a vowel other than *A.* The first name of **Ulysses S. Grant** is the only one among presidents that begins with a vowel other than *A.*

- *H* is the most popular first letter of presidential surnames—*Harrison, Hayes, Harrison, Harding,* and *Hoover. S* is the most common letter at the beginning of English words, but no president's surname starts with that letter.

- Only one president's name contains a letter that is found in no other president's name. That letter is the *q* in **John Quincy Adams.**

- **Ulysses Simpson Grant** and **Rutherford Birchard Hayes** are the only presidential names that contain *a, e, i, o,* and *u,* with a *y* to boot.

- Four presidents have had alliterative first and last names—**Woodrow Wilson, Calvin Coolidge, Herbert Hoover,** and **Ronald Reagan.** They all served in the twentieth century.

- **James Madison** is the only president whose first and last names alternate between consonants and vowels.

- A number of presidential last names can be charaded (cleft in two) to reveal two separate words:

Washington = *washing* + *ton*

Adams = *a* + *dams*

Jackson = *jack* + *son*

Fillmore = *fill* + *more*

Johnson = *john* + *son*

Hayes = *ha* + *yes*

Hoover = *ho* + *over*

Nixon = *nix* + *on*

Note that if you reverse the last two letters of **Richard Nixon**'s last name, you get a double negative—*nix* + *no.*

- Two presidents have had double letters in both their first and last names— **William Harrison** and **Millard Fillmore.**

- Four twentieth-century presidents have had surnames containing *oo*— **Roosevelt, Coolidge, Hoover,** and **Roosevelt.** All these men occupied the Oval Office in the first half of the twentieth century, three of them sequentially.

- Nine presidents with double letters in one of their names served sequentially—**William McKinley, Theodore Roosevelt, William Taft, Woodrow Wilson, Warren Harding, Calvin Coolidge, Herbert Hoover, Franklin Roosevelt,** and **Harry Truman.**

- Cleveland, McKinley, Roosevelt, Taft, and Wilson were elected sequentially and alphabetically.

- Taft and Nixon are the only presidential surnames that begin and end with the same letter. **Theodore Roosevelt** is the only U.S. president whose full name begins and ends with the same letter.

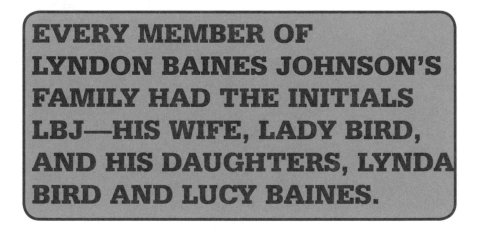

EVERY MEMBER OF LYNDON BAINES JOHNSON'S FAMILY HAD THE INITIALS LBJ—HIS WIFE, LADY BIRD, AND HIS DAUGHTERS, LYNDA BIRD AND LUCY BAINES.

- **Rutherford B. Hayes**'s first name contains the last name of **Gerald Ford.** **Andrew** and **Lyndon Johnson**'s last name contains the first name of four other presidents—Adams, Quincy Adams, Tyler, and Kennedy.

- *Pierce, Grant, Ford, Carter, Bush, Bush,* and (in Britain) *Hoover* are all common words when uncapitalized.

- Just as the word *president* is beheadable—*president* becomes *resident*—a number of presidential surnames transmogrify into new words when their first letters are lopped off:

Adams becomes *dams.*

Grant becomes *rant* becomes *ant.*

Hayes becomes *ayes* becomes *yes.*

Taft becomes *aft.*

CHAPTER XII
WHAT IT TAKES
TO BE PRESIDENT

AMERICAN PRESIDENTS have frequently commented on the joys and vicissitudes of their job. Judging by the utterances of some of our earliest chief executives, they did not take kindly to the position:

- "My movements to the chair of government," lamented **George Washington** in a letter, "will be accompanied by feelings not unlike those of a culprit who is going to the place of his execution." "No man who ever held the office of president would congratulate a friend on obtaining it," added **John Adams.**

- "No man will ever bring out of the Presidency the reputation which carries him into it. To myself, personally, it brings nothing but increasing drudgery and daily loss of friends," sighed **Thomas Jefferson,** who called the office "a splendid misery."

- The second **Adams, John Quincy,** echoed his father's disaffection with the office: "The four most miserable years of my life were my four years in the presidency."

- **Martin Van Buren** shrugged, "As to the presidency, the two happiest days of my life were those of my entrance upon the office and my surrender of it."

- Because of the U.S. Civil War, **James Buchanan** believed he would be the last president of the United States. Buchanan told

Lincoln, "My dear, sir, if you are as happy on entering the White House as I on leaving, you are a very happy man indeed."

- **Abraham Lincoln** may have said it best. When asked how it felt to be president, he explained: "You have heard about the man tarred and feathered and ridden out of town on a rail? A man in the audience asked him how he liked it, and his reply was that if it wasn't for the honor of the thing, he would much rather walk."

Later presidents have not been so dark in their assessments:

- "When you get to be President, there are all those things, the honors, the twenty-one gun salutes, all those things. You have to remember it isn't for you. It's for the Presidency," observed **Harry S. Truman.**

- **Lyndon Johnson** noted, "The presidency has made every man who occupies it, no matter how small, bigger than he was—and no matter how big he was, not big enough for its demands."

- **Ronald Reagan** smiled, "When I was announcing sports, I was happy and thought that was all I wanted out of life. Then came the chance at Hollywood, and that was even better. Now I'm doing something that makes everything else I've done seem dull as dishwater when I look back."

- "I enjoy being president!" **Theodore Roosevelt** yawped. "While president, I have been president emphatically!"

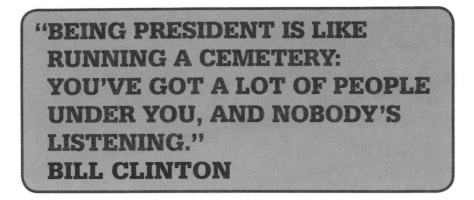

"BEING PRESIDENT IS LIKE RUNNING A CEMETERY: YOU'VE GOT A LOT OF PEOPLE UNDER YOU, AND NOBODY'S LISTENING."
BILL CLINTON

Many non-presidents have offered their wisdom about the presidency:

- I would rather be right than President. —*Henry Clay*

- Frankly, I don't mind not being President. I just mind that someone else is. —*Ted Kennedy*

- The presidency we get is the country we get. With each new president the nation is conformed spiritually. —*E. L. Doctorow*

- The President's decisions make the weather, and if he is great enough, change the climate, too. —*Theodore H. White*

- They pick a president and then for four years they pick on him. —*Adlai Stevenson*

- When I was a boy I was told that anybody could become President; I'm beginning to believe it. —*Clarence Darrow*

- The presidency is now a cross between a popularity contest and a high school debate, with an encyclopaedia of clichés the first prize. —*Saul Bellow*

- The office of the President is such a bastardizing thing, half royalty and half democracy, that nobody knows whether to genuflect or spit. —*Jimmy Breslin*

- You can fool some of the people all of the time, and all the people some of the time, which is just long enough to be president of the United States. —*Spike Milligan*

- Any American who is prepared to run for president should automatically, by definition, be disqualified from ever doing so. —*Gore Vidal*

"PRESIDENCY: THE GREASED PIG IN THE FIELD GAME OF AMERICAN POLITICS." AMBROSE BIERCE

CHAPTER XIII.
RUNNING MATES

CHESTER A. ARTHUR EXULTED that it was "a greater honor than I ever dreamed of attaining." Humorist Bill Vaughan called it "the last cookie on the plate. Everybody insists he won't take it, but somebody always does." They were talking about the vice presidency—that colorful, increasingly important, and routinely disparaged American political institution.

Others have been more blunt. **John Adams,** our first vice president, described the position as "the most insignificant that ever the imagination of man contrived or his imagination conceived."

"The vice presidency isn't worth a pitcher of warm spit." That was the advice **John Nance Garner,** vice president under Franklin D. Roosevelt, gave to **Lyndon Johnson,** a fellow Texan who had been asked by John F. Kennedy in 1960 to be Kennedy's running mate. Johnson accepted the offer and became president when Kennedy was assassinated.

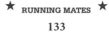

When asked if he might consider becoming vice president, war hero John McCain responded, "You know, I spent all those years in a North Vietnamese prison camp, kept in the dark, fed scraps—why the heck would I want to do that all over again?"

Under the original terms of the Constitution, the first vice presidents were the presidential candidates who placed second in the Electoral College, which voted for the office of President of the United States. Apparently, the signers of the Constitution believed that party politics would not interfere with the president and his vice president working together in exquisite harmony. Yeah, sure. In 1804, after a poisonous campaign between John Adams and his own vice president, **Thomas Jefferson,** the Twelfth Amendment required members of the Electoral College to vote separately for president and vice president.

Fourteen presidents have served as vice presidents—**John Adams, Thomas Jefferson, Martin Van Buren, John Tyler, Millard Fillmore, Andrew Johnson, Chester A. Arthur, Theodore Roosevelt, Calvin Coolidge, Harry S. Truman, Richard Nixon, Lyndon Johnson, Gerald Ford,** and **George H. W. Bush.**

You'd think, then, that a natural and common way to become president would be for a president and vice president to finish their terms naturally and for the vice president to run and win election as the next president.

In 1988, **George H. W. Bush** did just that, succeeding Ronald Reagan. But you have to go back more than a hundred and fifty years to find a vice president who became president immediately after his president voluntarily stepped aside. That man was **Martin Van Buren.** In 1836, Van Buren was elected president immediately following his term as vice president under Andrew Jackson.

The only other vice president/president who fits this pattern is **John Adams,** who succeeded George Washington. All three of these vice presidents who turned president immediately after their vice presidency—Adams, Van Buren, and Bush—lost their bids of reelection as president for a second term.

Here are some more fascinating facts about our vice presidents:

- For parts of their presidency or for their entire term, James Madison, Andrew Jackson, John Tyler, Millard Fillmore, Franklin Pierce, Andrew Johnson, Ulysses S. Grant, Theodore Roosevelt, Harry S. Truman, Lyndon Johnson, Richard Nixon, and Gerald Ford had no vice president.

AARON BURR, THOMAS JEFFERSON'S VICE PRESIDENT, FOUGHT PERHAPS THE MOST FAMOUS DUEL IN AMERICAN HISTORY.

- **Aaron Burr,** Thomas Jefferson's first vice president, fought perhaps the most famous duel in American history. A bitter political rival of Alexander Hamilton, Burr took umbrage at Hamilton's remarks at a dinner party. Burr challenged Hamilton to a duel and mortally wounded his rival in the exchange of gunfire. Burr was indicted for murder, and, although the charges were ultimately dismissed, he was driven from political life and the vice presidency.

- Can you think of the only other sitting vice president who shot a man? The answer is **Dick Cheney,** who, while shooting quail, accidentally peppered friend and attorney Harry Whittington with birdshot.

- **Elbridge Gerry,** a vice president to James Madison, is eponomously responsible for inspiring a political term in our English language. In 1812, in an effort to sustain his party's power, Governor Gerry divided the state of Massachusetts into electoral districts with more regard to politics than to geographical reality. It happened that one of the governor's manipulated districts resembled a salamander. Gilbert Stuart—the same fellow who had painted the famous portrait of George Washington—added a head, wings, and claws to a drawing of the district. According to one version of the story, Stuart exclaimed about his creation. "That looks like a salamander!" "No," riposted the editor of the newspaper in which the cartoon was to appear, "Better call it a Gerrymander!" The name *gerrymander* (now lower-cased and sounded with a soft *g*, even though Gerry's name began with a hard *g*) is still used today to describe the shaping of electoral entities for political gain.

- Seven vice presidents died in office—**George Clinton, Elbridge Gerry, William King, Henry Wilson, Thomas Hendricks, Garret Hobart,** and **James Sherman.** Only one president had two vice presidents die during his time in office. James Madison served two terms, and both times the man elected as his vice president died shortly after the beginning of the term—first, **George Clinton** and second, **Elbridge Gerry.**

SEVEN VICE PRESIDENTS DIED IN OFFICE.

- Two men have served as vice president under two different presidents— **George Clinton** (under Jefferson and Madison) and **John C. Calhoun** (Quincy Adams and Jackson).

- Two men resigned their vice presidency—**John C. Calhoun,** in 1832, to take a seat in the Senate—and **Spiro Agnew,** in 1973, upon pleading no contest to charges of accepting bribes while governor of Maryland.

- **John Tyler** was born in the same county as his president, William Henry Harrison—Charles City County, Virginia.

- **Charles Dawes,** vice president under Calvin Coolidge, composed a number of songs, including a well-known piece for violin, "Melody in A Minor." He also composed the popular song "It's All in the Game." In 1925, Dawes

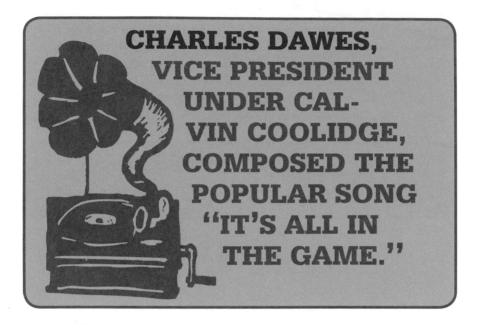

CHARLES DAWES, VICE PRESIDENT UNDER CALVIN COOLIDGE, COMPOSED THE POPULAR SONG "IT'S ALL IN THE GAME."

received the Nobel Peace Prize for his chairmanship of the Allied Reparation Commission and his origination of the Dawes Plan to facilitate Germany's payments of wartime debts.

- **Charles Curtis,** Herbert Hoover's running mate, is the only vice president of Native American ancestry. His mother was one-quarter Kaw, and he spent part of his early life on a Kaw reservation. Curtis, a great-great-grandson of White Plume, a Kansa-Kaw chief who had offered assistance to the Lewis and Clark expedition in 1804, was the only president or vice president of

Native American descent. He was also the last vice president (or president) to sport facial hair—in this case a mustache—while in office.

- Franklin D. Roosevelt is the only president to have had three vice presidents—**John Nance Garner, Henry A. Wallace,** and **Harry S. Truman.**

- When **John F. Kennedy** was told that he would have no trouble garnering the Democratic nomination for vice president, he quipped, "Let's not talk so much about vice. I'm against vice in any form."

- **Richard Nixon** completed his vice presidency in 1960 and was narrowly defeated by John F. Kennedy for the presidency. He was elected president eight years later. As such, he is the only vice president to become president after a gap between the two offices and the only twentieth-century president to win the office on his second try.

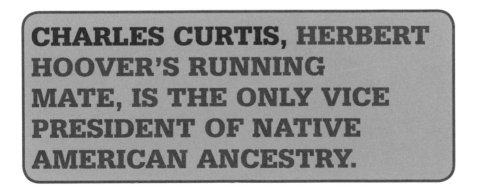

CHARLES CURTIS, HERBERT HOOVER'S RUNNING MATE, IS THE ONLY VICE PRESIDENT OF NATIVE AMERICAN ANCESTRY.

- "Nattering nabobs of negativism" may be the best-known turn of phrase associated with a vice president. **Spiro Agnew,** who served under Richard Nixon and who had a particularly acrimonious relationship with the press, employed this term in 1970 to refer to the members of the media. He also deemed the Fourth Estate "an effete corps of impudent snobs."

- In 2006, **Al Gore,** Bill Clinton's vice president, starred in an oscar-winning documentary feature film, *An Inconvenient Truth,* about global warming.

QUIZ

The following vice presidents, listed alphabetically by last name, never became president. Identify the president under whom each served:

1. Alben Barkley
2. George M. Dallas
3. Hannibal Hamlin
4. Hubert Humphrey
5. Thomas R. Marshall

6. Richard M. Johnson
7. Walter Mondale
8. Dan Quayle
9. Nelson Rockefeller
10. Adlai E. Stevenson

Answers:
1. Harry S. Truman | 2. James Polk | 3. Abraham Lincoln | 4. Lyndon Johnson | 5. Woodrow Wilson | 6. Martin Van Buren | 7. Jimmy Carter | 8. George H. W. Bush | 9. Gerald Ford | 10. Grover Cleveland

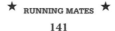

CHAPTER XIV.
FIRST LADIES RULE

WHAT IS UNUSUAL ABOUT THE FOLLOWING SENTENCE?:

FIRST LADIES RULE THE STATE
AND STATE THE RULE—"LADIES FIRST!"

Perhaps you noticed that, when read forward and backward word by word, the sentence comes out the same.

Many early first ladies expressed their own preference for how they were addressed, including the use of such titles as "Lady," "Queen," "Mrs. President," and "Mrs. Presidentress." **Martha Dandridge Custis Washington** was often referred to as "Lady Washington." The title "First Lady" first gained nationwide recognition in 1877, when newspaper journalist Mary C. Ames referred to **Lucy Webb Hayes** as "the first lady of the land" while reporting on the inauguration of Rutherford B. Hayes. Lucy Hayes was a tremendously popular First Lady, and the frequent reporting on her activities helped spread use of the title outside Washington.

Many first ladies have not liked the title "First Lady" but this has not stopped them from making their marks on history in diverse ways:

- **Abigail Smith Adams** and **Barbara Pierce Bush** are the only two women to have been both the wife of a president and the mother of another president. But Barbara Pierce Bush possesses another distinction. She is also a descendant of Thomas Pierce, an ancestor of Franklin Pierce. Barbara Bush is a great-great-great-niece and a fourth cousin four times removed of President Pierce. Barbara Bush once quipped, "Somewhere out there in this audience may even be someone who will one day follow in my footsteps and preside over the White House as the president's spouse. I wish him well."

- **Dolley Paine Todd Madison** often acted as the official hostess during Thomas Jefferson's administration as well as that of her husband. She was thus a President's White House hostess for sixteen years, an accomplishment unmatched by any other woman in American history.

- When British troops burned the White House in 1814, **Dolley Madison** courageously rescued Gilbert

Stuart's famous portrait of George Washington before she fled the city. That most recognized of all presidential portraits is the only remaining possession from the original building.

- **Martha Wayles Skelton Jefferson** and **Hannah Hoes Van Buren** both died eighteen years before their husbands were elected presidents of the United States. Daughter **Polly Jefferson Randolph** on occasion served as hostess at the White House, as did daughter-in-law **Angelica Singleton Van Buren.** In his autobiography, Van Buren never once mentions his wife.

- After the death of James Polk at the age of fifty-three, his widow, **Sarah Childress Polk,** dressed in mourning for the rest of her life.

- Millard Fillmore was the only president to marry his schoolteacher—**Abigail Powers.** Two years younger than she, Fillmore was her student at New Hope Academy. Abigail was responsible for the installation of the first bathtub in the Executive Mansion, an act for which she incurred severe public criticism. Bathtubs have been a White House fixture ever since.

- During the term of James Buchanan, our only bachelor president, his niece, **Harriet Lane,** played the role of First Lady.

- Andrew Johnson married **Eliza McCardle** in 1827 when she was just seventeen years of age.

- Rutherford B. and **Lucy Hayes** banned all forms of alcohol at presidential gatherings and functions. For this action the first lady earned the nickname

"Lemonade Lucy." A sideboard that had been presented to "Lemonade Lucy" Hayes by the Women's Christian Temperance Union was purchased by a Washington saloonkeeper. He prominently displayed the sideboard in his barroom on Pennsylvania Avenue, loaded with liquors.

- Like James Buchanan, Grover Cleveland entered the White House as a bachelor. At the age of forty-nine, President Cleveland married twenty-one-year-old **Frances Folsom** in the Blue Room of the White House. Frances became the youngest of all first ladies, and the couple's baby, Ruth, was the first child born in the White House. When, in 1889, her husband was voted out of office after his first term, **Frances Folsom Cleveland** told the staff to take care of the furniture because they would return. She was right.

- **Edith Kermit Carow Roosevelt,** first lady at the turn of the last century, managed the White House while raising six children.

- In 1912, **Helen Herron Taft,** popularly known as "Nellie," supervised the planting of the famous Washington cherry trees, a gift from the people of Tokyo.

- **Edith Bolling Galt Wilson** has been called "the secret president" and "the first woman to run the government." This legend arose from her perceived role in affairs of state after Woodrow Wilson suffered a prolonged and debilitating illness. Edith was Woodrow's constant attendant and took over many routine duties of government. But she did not try to control the executive branch. In her 1939 *My Memoir*, she writes: "So began my stewardship. I studied every paper, sent from the different Secretaries or senators, and tried to digest and

EDITH BOLLING GALT WILSON HAS BEEN CALLED "THE SECRET PRESIDENT."

present in tabloid form the things that, despite my vigilance, had to go to the President. I myself never made a single decision regarding the disposition of public affairs. The only decision that was mine was what was important and what was not, and the very important decision of when to present matters to my husband." Edith Wilson died on December 28, 1961, the anniversary of Woodrow's birth.

- **(Anna) Eleanor Roosevelt** broke precedent to hold press conferences, travel to all parts of the country, give lectures and radio broadcasts, and express her opinions candidly in a daily syndicated newspaper column, "My Day."

- When **Eleanor Roosevelt** informed Truman that her husband, Franklin, had died, Truman asked, "Is there anything I can do for you?" Shaking her head, Mrs. Roosevelt said, "Is there anything we can do for you? For you are the one in trouble now."

- Being from the Midwest, Harry S. Truman often talked to farm groups. Whenever he held forth about fertilizer, Truman used the word *manure*, much to the embarrassment of his support staff. Finally, the public relations people went to **Bess Truman** to ask her help in getting her husband to stop

using the offending word. She sighed, "You'd be amazed how long it took me to get him to start using *manure.*"

- **Hillary Rodham Clinton** is the first and only first lady to be elected to high office, as senator from New York. As of the writing of this book, she is a candidate for President of the United States. She is also the only first lady to have earned a law degree—from Yale Law School, where she met her future husband.

> # HILLARY RODHAM CLINTON IS THE FIRST AND ONLY FIRST LADY TO BE ELECTED TO HIGH OFFICE.

QUIZ

Here, alphabetically by first name, are the names sixteen first ladies had before they hooked up with presidents. Identify each president to whom they were married.

1. Claudia (Lady Bird) Taylor
2. Elizabeth (Betty) Bloomer
3. Ellen Louise Axson
4. Elizabeth Kortright
5. Elizabeth (Bess) Virginia Wallace
6. Jacqueline (Jackie) Lee Bouvier
7. Julia Dent
8. Julia Gardiner
9. Laura Welch
10. Letitia Christian
11. Lou Henry
12. Mamie Geneva Doud
13. Mary Todd
14. Nancy Davis
15. Thelma Catherine Ryan (Pat)
16. Rosalynn Smith

Answers

1. Lyndon Johnson | 2. Gerald Ford | 3. Woodrow Wilson | 4. James Monroe | 5. Harry S. Truman | 6. John F. Kennedy | 7. Ulysses S. Grant | 8. John Tyler | 9. George W. Bush | 10. John Tyler | 11. Herbert Hoover | 12. Dwight Eisenhower | 13. Abraham Lincoln | 14. Ronald Reagan | 15. Richard Nixon | 16. Jimmy Carter

RICHARD LEDERER is the author of more than thirty books about language, history, and humor. His syndicated column, "Looking at Language," appears in newspapers and magazines throughout the United States. He has been profiled in magazines as diverse as *The New Yorker, People,* and *The National Enquirer* and frequently appears on public and commercial radio. Dr. Lederer has been elected International Punster of the Year and Toastmasters International Golden Gavel winner. He lives with his wife, Simone van Egeren, in San Diego.